Dedication

To every young man I ever coached. Each of you, in some way, has helped make me the man I am today. Thank you.

WE KICK BALLS: TRUE STORIES FROM THE YOUTH SOCCER WARS

TABLE OF CONTENTS

INTRODUCTION

Lou Gehrig once said he was the luckiest man on the face of the earth. But he died shortly thereafter, leaving his spot open for someone else to claim.

I'll take it.

Lou was a baseball player, of course, and I'm a soccer guy, and that sums up life from the mid-20th century through the beginning of the 21st. Soccer has overtaken baseball as *the* American youth sport. Far more kids play soccer today than baseball (as the baseball philosopher Casey Stengel said, "You could look it up"). More dads are teaching their children to shoot on goal than throw curveballs (to the delight of pediatricians everywhere). And moms have gotten into the act too, unlike Little League where the job of the woman is to man the concession booth.

Which is why this book is about soccer, not baseball.

I consider myself lucky to have grown up in Westport, Connecticut, a town that embraced soccer so early and strongly that as a fifth grader in the mid-1960s I had the chance to play in a recreational league, then interscholastically in junior high. I consider myself lucky that at Staples High School I was a bit player in the legendary program pioneered by Albie Loeffler, one of those quiet but brilliant men whose influence on the game has been both profound and overlooked. I consider myself lucky that the college I attended, Brown University, had one of the top soccer teams in the country. I was nowhere near good enough to play, but I covered the squad for the newspaper and continued my love affair with the game. I consider myself lucky to have been befriended by two other quiet but passionate men, Jim Kuhlmann and Jim Kaufman, at

3

whose Soccer Farm camp I worked for many years, and where I learned much of what I know – about soccer and life.

I consider myself lucky to have returned to Westport after college, and been able to help organize the Westport Soccer Association. I consider myself lucky to have coached one or two WSA teams each season for two decades; that on-field success pales in comparison with the off-field capers, hi-jinks and adventures I have been privileged to share with hundreds of players, their parents, and assorted siblings, relatives, friends and hangers-on. I consider myself lucky to be coaching now at my alma mater, Staples High School, doing my bit to continue the tremendous soccer tradition that has endured there for over 50 years.

I consider myself lucky that I have made part of my living writing about soccer, and that I have been able to give something back to the game by volunteering as a coach and administrator for so long (this being youth soccer, I now get paid). I consider myself lucky that soccer has allowed me to meet amazing people and have incredible experiences in places as diverse as Brazil, Iceland, Italy and New Zealand. I consider myself lucky to be able to write a book like this, about all my experiences – the good, the bad and the ugly; the highs and lows; the celebrations and funerals, and of course the wins and losses (even though the games themselves form a minor part of it all).

I consider myself very, very lucky that many years ago I could fully acknowledge who I am, with virtually no repercussions, in an arena (the sports world) that many still call "the last closet."

Mostly, though, I consider myself lucky that I am still relatively young, and look forward to many more years enjoying the greatest game on earth.

Two final notes: Nearly all the names of players and parents have been changed, to protect both the innocent and the guilty. The only exceptions are Scott, who was killed in the World Trade Center on September 11, 2001; Preston, who died of an undiagnosed heart condition; Michael, who died in a freak soccer accident, and Dick, a parent who also died far too young. It is important to honor their memories with their real names.

And yes, all the stories are completely true. Or, at least, I've told them the way I remember them.

Dan Woog
Westport, Connecticut
August 2012

PS: *Huge* props to Jason Tillotson (my fantastically talented web and cover designer; contact information: jt.design.10@gmail.com), and Christian Abraham, the Connecticut Post staff photographer whose great photo of James Hickok graces the book cover.

PPS: Want to know more about the Staples High School soccer program? Check out www.StaplesSoccer.com.

MY $25,000 CAR WASH, MY 48-HOUR FLIGHT TO BRAZIL, AND OTHER WILDLY IMPROBABLE YET INCREDIBLY TRUE SOCCER STORIES

Sometimes – don't ask me why – I went on a soccer trip without being in charge. For a control freak like me, it was like skydiving without a parachute. Neither event is particularly wise or comfortable.

One such trip was with the Westport Strikers, a team that gave new meaning to the word "crazed." The players were fine, mind you; it was the parents who were a bit, shall we say, over-involved. Unfortunately, you could not separate the kids from the grownups. That was not the youngsters' fault; their parents simply would not allow it. Nearly all the boys were first-born children; it was the mid-'80s, when Ronald Reagan railed against the excesses of '60s parental permissiveness, and the stock market sizzled.

The connection between stocks and soccer was important to the Strikers. Coach Toby Jackson worked on Wall Street as a portfolio manager for three or four fabulously wealthy clients. So after moving several million dollars of money around each morning, he had tons of time on his hands. For several years, he devoted every second of that free time to soccer.

Toby started out knowing less about soccer than a forsythia bush. But he applied his MBA-trained mind to the game as if it were a particularly intriguing hedge fund. He read every soccer book ever published. He toured the country seeking courses and clinics. He hired specialists – shooting coaches, goalkeeping gurus, throw-in experts – to work with his team, and in the process tutor him.

And Toby asked questions. Christ almighty, did he ask questions. Following a particularly tough loss – or an easy win, or close tie; the result did not matter – Toby would call. He phoned me, he phoned the high school varsity coach, for all I know he phoned Manchester United. He wanted to know what he did right, what he did wrong, what he could have done differently the previous day – on every play. Had Toby been involved in football, Vince Lombardi would have declared him out of control.

And nearly all the other parents were even more over the top than Toby.

Many were high-powered executives. If the business ideal is that the guy who dies with the most toys wins, then their goal in soccer became to die with the most wins. That attitude permeated everything they did. Whatever the Strikers attempted, it had to be "better" or "more" than any other team.

Which is how they ran a $25,000 car wash.

To raise money for their European trip – a noble concept, because most of the parents could simply have chartered individual jets – the Striker fathers devised the mother of all fundraisers. A car wash with more angles than a Picasso painting, it went like this:

In early spring the players knocked on doors, seeking pledges based on the number of cars they would wash. Friends, neighbors, relatives, teachers and random supermarket strangers signed up to donate a certain amount – five cents, ten cents, a quarter – for every vehicle to be washed. Every person who pledged was promised a free car wash. (In typical Striker fashion, the players underwent "training sessions" in effective sales techniques before hitting the streets. Jehovah's Witnesses, take note.)

On the Sunday of the event, the parking lot looked like an aircraft carrier flight deck. Parents directed cars into five well-marked lanes. Waiting their turns, drivers were handed flyers describing the upcoming trip. Children received lollipops; a disc jockey blared music. There was no set price for the car wash; "donations" were "encouraged," which meant most people gave more than the usual $5 (many of those who had been promised a free wash by pledging ponied up too). Squadrons of car-washers – players, dads, moms, siblings, friends and anyone else who had been shanghaied into duty – worked with fevered intensity, overseen by parental supervisors. A large tote board at the exit recorded the number of cars washed.

The grand total was 538. Some people had been suckered into pledging $1 a car; in a show of compassion, car wash leaders decreed that due to the enormous number of vehicles, folks owing sums equivalent to their mortgage payment could give whatever they felt comfortable with. In all, over $25,000 was raised.

And that was just one Strikers project.

Naturally, when the day came to head to Europe (following a special session where business travelers gave special lessons in packing suitcases – I can't make this stuff up), an enormous entourage gathered. They were there not to see the boys off, but to accompany them.

The 14 players were joined by 17 "others": mothers, fathers, sisters, brothers. No one brought a maid, though I'm sure the thought crossed several families' minds. Had this been the 1800s, they would have commandeered a private rail car.

It turned into the oddest soccer trip I've ever been on, because time and again the focus shifted from the players to the hangers-on. The goalkeeper played his worst game immediately after his mother tripped leaving the bus, breaking her ankle. Players ate not before matches but after, because that was more convenient (and vacation-like) for parents. The woman videotaping the trip was in Cecil B. DeMille mode, so at times getting the right camera angle became more important than whatever was happening in real time. I fully expected her to stop a game and demand that a Striker striker score again, because she'd missed the shot. One mother decided to take her son sightseeing alone. She said he was sick, then took off merrily with him.

Happily, the boys managed to have a great time despite the cloying presence of parents, who in my mind (you must know by now) defeat the purpose of an overseas trip for kids. In Southend, England, the kids made such an impression on the host Benfleet Soccer Club that when the farewell party broke up – after the English and American boys joined together in an impromptu cheer – the Benfleet players formed a double line and applauded as the Westporters walked through. Lads on both teams were crying.

(The scene was a bit different two nights earlier, after a dance at a local hall when the Strikers' bus was chased by a swarm of screaming, sobbing British girls. "I feel like the Beatles," said one of our players, who I am sure could not have identified any of the Fab Four on a bet.)

In Stukenbrock, Germany a planning snafu meant that a few boys ended up in home stays by themselves, with families that spoke little English. The Westport parents leaped to solve that "problem." They wanted to rent hotel rooms, hire English-speaking hosts, do whatever they could in their businesslike, action plan-oriented way. I have no idea how, but I finally convinced them the situation was okay. This was not what the boys had expected, but hey, sometimes in life things happen. It was like soccer: They would adapt and survive.

You know what? They did. The Strikers learned sign language. They breakfasted on cold cuts with chocolate sprinkles. And they discovered they could have a good time even if their parents were not joined at their hips, micromanaging every move.

As for coach Toby, he flourished too. His boys won four games, tied four and lost only one. And he found a whole new continent of experts to ask questions of.

Speaking of new continents, for sheer adventure nothing – *nothing* – beats my trip to Brazil.

Unfortunately, much of the excitement took place during the two days it took to get there.

Brazil is less than 10 hours by air from New York. If you stop somewhere, add another couple of hours. Because the flight is south, not east or west, the time change is negligible; two hours, no jet lag. Flying to South America should be easier than driving to South Carolina.

Unless you are going to check out the first (and, it turned out, only) Pele Tournament.

Hey, it sounded good on paper.

I was invited to join an elite group of soccer writers (including Lynn Berling Manuel, editor of *Soccer America* magazine, and Paul Gardner, curmudgeonly columnist for the same publication) on a journey to Sao Paulo and Rio. Some of Brazil's most famous soccer folks, such as Professor Julio Mazzei -- Pele's irrepressible major domo -- were launching what they hoped would be a flagship youth tournament. They were eager to divert some of the many American soccer dollars – I mean, teams – from Europe to South America, and we journalists were offered a free trip to see the attractions for ourselves.

We saw more than we bargained for.

The journey began inauspiciously. A gas leak roused me from my home at 2:45 a.m., so I was already tired when I boarded my flight to Orlando to join the other writers, and four youth teams. I arrived at mid-morning, right on time, only to be met by many serious faces.

"There seems to be a little problem," said one of the Pele Tournament representatives. "There may be a slight delay."

Those two phrases – "little problem" and "slight delay" – foreshadowed what was to come. The slight delay arose because the plane we were supposed to use was not quite ready. How could it be? It was still in Brazil.

I could not imagine a worse fate than to be stuck in an airport for what any sentient individual could tell would be more than a "slight delay." Eight hours seemed more like it. So a pair of fellow scribes and I rented a car, then set out to see the sights. Disney World seemed a stretch — by the time we got there, parked, forked over the usurious ticket price and joined one line it would be time to return — so we opted for Orlando's other attractions. We visited Sea World, Parrot World, Monkey World, Gator World, Geezer World, and just about every other World we could find. Finally at dusk, laden with postcards — and having spent far more than even a day at Disney World costs — we returned to the airport.

The players on the four teams had spent their day juggling soccer balls, drinking Cokes and discussing how much the trip sucked so far. The adults had a far more constructive way of amusing themselves: the bar. It was quite a crew that got ready, at 7 p.m., to board the aircraft.

I was thrilled to be bumped up to first class. Visions of a luxurious night, and an easy sleep, filled my tired head. But the Pan Am plane looked a bit small for such a long haul. It was — as I learned when they announced that our destination was Miami.

Miami! We were not even leaving the state! We could have walked there from Orlando, had we forgone Sea, Parrot, Monkey and Etc. Worlds!

I enjoyed my first class flight, all 12 minutes of it, then settled in to await the final leg. Of course, there was a little problem, causing a slight delay of only a couple of hours. The players did what they did best — juggling soccer balls, drinking Cokes and bitching — while the parents, having not had a drink for at least 45 minutes, repaired to the bar.

I looked out the window at the tarmac, and saw our next plane. It was big and colorful. It looked like it could fly anywhere. But the side read Air Jamaica. Hmmm, I asked myself, how can Air Jamaica fly from Miami to Sao Paulo? I had a sneaking suspicion we would make a pit stop along the way.

How wrong I was. We did not stop briefly in Jamaica; we stopped there to deplane. Actually, we stopped in two separate places. First we landed in Montego Bay to off-load two of the teams; the rest of us continued on to Kingston. That was not a long flight, true, but the Jamaicans didn't have the taxiing concept down real well, so we sat for, oh, an hour or so on the runway.

Which meant we landed in Kingston at 2 a.m. I probably should have mentioned that this was the weekend of a Jamaican national holiday – Independence Day, a biggie – so we were not the only plane arriving at the airport, even at such an odd hour.

In fact, once we got off the airplane we were herded through the terminal as if our (soccer) balls were radioactive. "You must hurry! Keep moving, please! A 747 is arriving right behind you!" customs agents shouted. We did not know if that plane was headed for the customs line itself – which, given the decrepit state of the airport, was quite possible – or whether the authorities simply wanted to clear space for the next load of passengers. At any rate we tried to comply, but it was difficult. Every inch of floor space was occupied by either 1) newly arriving Jamaicans wheeling luggage carts filled with televisions, washing machines and every other electrical possession they owned or 2) rats. Okay, I exaggerate about the rats. We saw only three of them.

But move we did, and eventually we were herded into a crowded shuttle bus. That, to me, was a clear sign we were not going to Brazil any time soon. It was 2:30 a.m., but even in my befogged state I knew that no roads lead from Kingston to Sao Paulo.

Instead we were driven – rapidly, insanely and loudly – through the streets of Kingston to a hotel on the outskirts of the city. It might actually have been beyond the outskirts; perhaps it was back in Montego Bay itself. Wherever it was, it took 45 minutes to get there. We were all grateful to arrive safely, for by that time everyone was beyond exhausted. We looked forward to a few hours sleep. But that was a dream, because on Jamaican Independence Day it is a tradition to play music in the streets all night long. The favorite spot is right underneath my hotel window.

So you can imagine our mood when we reassembled back at the Kingston airport the next morning for our flight to god knows where. Unfortunately, there was a little problem, causing a slight delay of a mere three hours. Finally, however, our VASP plane appeared. It was the same one that had been stuck in Brazil, when we were in Orlando. None of us had ever heard of VASP. But this plane had wings, windows, a tail and cockpit, and it appeared ready to do something neither Pan Am nor Air Jamaica had done: fly to Sao Paulo.

And it fully intended to do so, except for one small problem: The president of Mexico had just arrived in Jamaica on state business, causing a slight delay. All air traffic was halted. Hey, at least I got to see a 21-gun salute. And had time to buy a T-shirt that said, "Jamaica. No problem."

Long after 3 p.m. I boarded the plane in a state that hovered between amazement and disbelief. I was in awe I was finally going to get to Brazil, but stunned I would have to do it in an aircraft that seemed configured to hold the entire population of the country, with half of Uruguay thrown in. Seats were everywhere: six on each side, eight across the middle. Jump seats folded out from the wall, and I believe a few more were tucked in the overhead bins.

I settled in to my aisle seat. I glanced up, only to see the fattest human being on the planet aiming straight for the empty one next to me.

I was as tired as I've ever been, but my primal self-preservation reflex kicked in. I turned to the boy sitting across the aisle. He was 14, a member of the Dallas Longhorns team traveling with us. I'd been intrigued by these Longhorns. They looked just like the Westport boys I'd coached, except for the 10-gallon hats and cowboy boots. We had not been formally introduced, but there was no time to spare.

"Sit here!" I commanded.

The Longhorn – accustomed, I suppose, to obeying his elders – did as he was told. He got up and moved next to me. The fat man waddled closer, and leaned his blubbery body over both of us. "I think you're in my seat," he said to the boy next to me.

"Well, we're together on this soccer trip," I said. "Do you mind sitting there?" I motioned to the now-empty seat across the aisle.

"No problem!" the man said.

It was a fortuitous move. Dennis turned out to be a bright kid, with the same interests in writing and politics as I. We had a great plane ride (and continued corresponding long after the Brazil trip was over). We enjoyed each other's company so much, we would barely have noticed that the smoking section was on the left hand side of the plane – not the back, as was normal in those smoking-is-legal days – if the air had not circulated clockwise, right into our noses.

Of course, we had miles to go before we slept, or reached Sao Paulo for that matter. The plane flew and flew and flew. VASP engines are not particularly powerful, I guess, especially when the plane is crammed with thousands of people. At long last, in the middle of the night – our second night – we landed.

In Manaus.

I consider myself a pretty worldly guy, but never in my life had I heard of Manaus. Neither had anyone else in our traveling party. The Brazilians, however, knew it well. "It is in the middle of the Amazon!" they informed us. And sure enough, it is. We could tell, because on our descent into the airport we saw many, many lights in the city – and then they ended. Just like that. They did not taper off; they simply stopped.

"That's odd," I said out loud.

"That is the jungle," someone said. It's a good thing we did not overshoot the runway; otherwise, I am sure, crocodiles would have eaten the entire VASP plane, thousands of Brazilians and Urugayans and Americans and all.

Finally we took off again, and made it to Rio by 2 a.m. Unfortunately, that was not our ultimate destination; Sao Paulo was. So after a hop, skip and a jump south – hey, what's another hour, when you've already spent 48 or so – we landed at what flight attendants call "your final destination." Bedraggled, sleep-deprived, smelly, unshaven (for by this time even the 14-year-olds had grown facial hair, and were working on full beards) and disoriented, we hauled ourselves off the plane.

There to greet us was Professor Mazzei. He exuded hospitality. He wore a smile the size of the man who'd tried to sit next to me on the VASP plane, and looked like he had not a care in the world. Judging by Professor Mazzei, we'd taxied in a few minutes ahead of schedule.

"Welcome to Brazil!" he said, in that Portuguese-flavored accent that can make even the most mundane statement sound impossibly exotic. "Did you have a good flight?"

Somehow, from a man called "the professor," it sounded like the dumbest thing I ever heard.

Although this was August, it was Brazil – and south of the equator, that means winter. Besides, it was 6:45 a.m. The taxi driver wore a scarf. For breakfast, we were served chicken soup. Welcome to Brazil indeed!

The food got better – I particularly loved the melons, fried bananas, beef and juices -- and the rest of the trip proceeded (relatively) more smoothly. Sao Paulo will never be confused with the Garden of Eden, but the rest of the country is exotic, sensual, alive and beautiful, and the opportunities for unique soccer experiences unparalleled.

One of the most telling events happened soon after a game in which the Longhorns – the team I adopted – lost to a local club. The players returned to the hotel, nursing their hurt pride – with typical teenage Texas swagger they thought they could beat anyone, even *Brazilians* – and found the entrance blocked by street urchins. They offered to shine the boys' soccer shoes. The price was 10 *cruzados*, which worked out to a little under two cents. The Americans, humbled and embarrassed, gave them two dollars.

Equally disconcerting were scenes I've never found in the United States: miles upon miles of *favelas*, tin and cardboard shacks in which enormous families live with no sanitation, privacy or comfort, but somehow they keep their dignity intact. I saw very few beggars; rather, I saw Brazilian men walking miles to work, women sweeping dirt out of their shanties, all of them smiling through it all.

We took a side trip through breathtaking mountains and past horrendous *favelas* to Santos, the seaside city where Pele got his start. As a special treat we were invited to his nearby home, a modest little place featuring a swimming pool, fountains, waterfalls, a chapel, an exotic bird aviary, a rooftop tennis court, screening and game rooms, tons of art, soccer goals (naturally) and a bazillion trophies. He was away at the time, which made me feel like an intruder. An excited one, but an intruder nonetheless.

The journalists spent a day in Belo Horizonte, the dusty city where in 1950 the United States shocked the entire globe (except the U.S., which could not have cared less) by defeating England 1-0 in the World Cup. Wilf Mannion, a member of that English team, was with us, as were Harry Keough and Walter Bahr, who played for the U.S. squad. All three received royal treatment. "Belo" is just a footnote to soccer history, but walking the grounds where such an amazing event occurred – with Wilf, Harry, Walter, local press and dignitaries, several fans who had actually been there, and an entourage of charming neighborhood children – was indeed memorable. There was slight disagreement between the two Americans and the Englishman as to exactly how Joe Gaetjens' lone goal was scored (no film exists of the shot), but no one felt shy about demonstrating his version.

Harry and Walter proved to be excellent traveling companions. One of my most vivid memories is of a moonlit night, long after dinner. Several youngsters kicked a ragged ball in the street, just like old-timers say they used to. Harry and Walter, both in their 60s, joined them, holding their own and even showing off a few smooth moves. The Brazilian youths had no idea they were knocking around with two United States legends – nor would they have cared -- but for an American coach and fan like me, it was a sight to behold.

Equally memorable, though for a different reason, was the day the four teams – in addition to the Longhorns, there was one from Virginia, one from Long Island, and a third I can't even remember – compared notes. They were discussing the ups and downs of the first (and, it turned out, only) Pele Tournament, when the talk turned to money. Somehow it came out that the Longhorns and two other squads were being comped; their costs were covered, in hopes they would spread the good word and return the following year with many more teams in tow. The fourth team, however, had paid its own way – the only one to do so. Understandably, from then on that group took a somewhat dimmer view of the "little problems" that popped up several dozen times a day.

But problems became easier to overlook once we were in Rio. (The writers took a half-hour flight from Sao Paulo, which set us back $33, while the four soccer teams trundled there by bus. We tried to feel sympathy when the coaches described the trek in a bus without heat in the 40-degree night, but it was tough to look concerned while smirking.) We stayed in a luxurious hotel across from the beach, where the swimwear could best be described as "dental floss." We watched Vasco da Gama beat Flamengo 1-0 to win the Rio de Janeiro league championship match at Maracana, the storied, crumbling stadium that seats well over 150,000 yet has – as the women traveling with us discovered – bathrooms serving approximately two females. (If it was any consolation, we told them, the guys' facilities were not much better.) The game itself was great, but the atmosphere – samba dancing from start to finish, smoke bombs in both teams' colors, confetti streamers, gigantic flags, hot air balloons and raucous cheering -- had to be seen, heard and smelled to be believed.

Late in the match someone hurled a live chicken from the upper deck. It landed not far from us, many feet below. What was most remarkable was not that it occurred; it was that someone had actually brought a chicken into the stadium, held onto it for several hours, then decided to fling it overboard. Unfazed, the chicken flapped its wings and strutted away.

The Longhorns, my adopted team, did North America proud by playing several Rio teams, representing world-famous clubs like Flamengo, Vasco da Gama and Botofogo, close. Pele finally showed up, and the Longhorns presented him with a cowboy hat. Gamely he put it on. Displaying the patience of Job and the dignity of Mother Theresa, he then posed for 172,000 photos.

We spent several joyful days touring Rio's magnificent sights. I was particularly taken with the funicular ride up Corcovado to the statue of Christ the Redeemer and Sugar Loaf, part of the mountains that sweep right down to the ocean. Though it was winter, with temperatures "only" in the low 80s, the beaches lived up to their legendary reputation. The surf roared in; a cast of healthy-looking men and boys played soccer and volleyball, ran and did acrobatics on the sand from dawn until way past dusk, while the women -- no matter what their age -- looked stunningly elegant. Rio is truly a special city, and I will be forever grateful that soccer was the vehicle that brought me there. (Metaphorically speaking, of course; actually an excruciating series of Pan Am, Air Jamaica and VASP planes did the trick.)

The return trip was much simpler. I wangled a non-stop flight, Rio to New York. In nine hours I was home, and the Pan Am seats were spacious enough that I did not have to worry about an obese man trying to wedge in next to me. It was almost too easy.

Then there was Barcelona.

By that point I had mellowed considerably – and of course, I was in charge. Almost anything that could happen on a trip had already happened, and the players always managed to emerge alive (if not always unscathed). They solved problems (see the chapter called "It's All About Problem Solving"). They learned a bit about themselves, and a lot about the world; they gained confidence, which was not only a joy to see, but carried over to the soccer field as well. Somehow, we always managed to return home with roughly the same number of boys we brought.

Barcelona came at the end of a long but thoroughly delightful trip. We had a great home stay in Germany. We won the Italy Cup in the funky seaside resort city of Rimini. Then in Spain we made a strong run at the Copa Catalunya – and, much to our players' amazement, added the Fair Play Trophy to our stash.

We were staying on a college campus an hour north of the city. It was a great setup. Four boys shared suites, each with its own living room and kitchenette. (The 16- and 17-year-olds could not prepare anything more exotic than cereal and cheese, though they made pathetic attempts at cooking spaghetti and eggs.) But a college outside of Barcelona is not *Barcelona*, and after we spent a free day and night there they realized exactly what they were missing. I thought I was being pretty lenient – because the clubs don't open until midnight (!), I let them stay until 2 a.m. – but this particular group, if you gave them a centimeter they wanted a kilometer. And there were several boys who argued quite persuasively that they deserved the whole nine yards.

On our second to last night in Spain, their lawyer-in-training spokesman pointed out that I had always said if they showed they could handle freedom, I'd give them more. (True.) They'd done all I'd asked on the field. (Absolutely – far more, in fact.) The soccer part of the journey was over; there was nothing to rest up for. *Pleasepleaseplease* couldn't they have one last night in Barcelona?

There was one small problem. Our bus driver had the night off, and the last train back to our college stopped running at midnight – precisely the time the clubs flung open their doors. The next train – the first of the morning – left at 5 a.m. Their solution: They promised to be on that one. They absolutely, positively would stay out no later than 5.

There was a time when I would have joined them in Barcelona, but that time was back in the 20th century. I wanted my sleep – I had stayed up late for two weeks now, and we had a 4 a.m. departure the morning after next – so I was not about to wait up all night for them. At the same time, it would have been unfair to prevent them from creating one final night of stories to bring home to their friends simply because I wanted some shuteye.

So, against my better judgment – I told you they argued well – I agreed to their all-night trip to Barcelona. However, I set certain conditions. One was that they all carry train, city and area maps, and show me their maps before they left (and prove they could read them). The second condition was that they slip a note with their names under my door as soon as they returned, so when I awoke I would not worry about who had or had not made it back. And I told them they always had to be with someone; there would be no going off alone.

The third condition was, of course, impossible to verify. For all I know they split up the instant they walked to the train station.

The first condition was met – sort of. Groups of boys entered my suite, earnestly pulled out their maps and demonstrated a passing knowledge of map-reading. We talked about the dangers of being an American in a large, unfamiliar city. I congratulated myself on covering as many bases as I could. Not until later – an hour or so after they left – did I discover most of their maps still on my kitchen table. Our talks had been so mesmerizing, I guess, they completely forgot them.

Two boys out of the 15 – both older, and leaders -- decided not to go. They said they were too tired; besides, they had girlfriends back home and were not interested in going clubbing "and whatever." I have no idea whether that was the whole story or if I was missing some subtext, but it was not my place to pry. The three of us had a nice dinner at a fancy restaurant. Then they did their wash and went to sleep. I did my administrative work, and went to sleep too.

At 2:30 a.m., my phone rang. It was the mother of a player. She needed to talk with him, to iron out details about getting home from the airport.

"Ummm....he's not here right now," I said hesitantly.

"Where is he?" she asked, logically enough.

"Well....they're in Barcelona," I said.

There was a pause.

"What time is it over there?" I calculated quickly – it was 8:30 p.m. back in Connecticut.

"It's – 2:30," I said. I hoped she wouldn't catch on.

She did. "2:30 a.m.?" she wondered.

"Uh, yeah."

There was another pause, far longer than the first. I conjured up mental images: She was writing a petition to get me fired. She was figuring out the quickest way to call the Spanish police. She was passed out on the floor.

Finally she spoke. "Wow!" she said in a voice far kinder than I had any right to expect. "I wish you were my mommy!"

THEY ARE THE CHAMPIONS

Pure joy.

That's an odd emotion to feel when your team ends its season with a devastating loss. In the case of the 2006 Staples High School boys soccer team, that meant a 2-1 golden-goal overtime defeat in the state championship match. After a thrilling run to the finals – including 12 straight games without a loss, nine consecutive shutouts and five overtime matches, two of which went to the second round of penalty kicks – we finally ran out of gas.

Less than 25 minutes from the end – when we could almost taste victory, hoisting the school's 12th state title trophy as the players took their last, well-deserved cool-down run – Simsbury, our very worthy opponent, tied the score. And then, in overtime, they stunned us with a spectacular goal. A seeing-eye shot lofted lazily over everyone before nestling in the far netting. The improbable finish set off a frenzied celebration by the Trojans, while Staples players slumped to the ground in utter misery.

I felt as bad for them as they did for themselves – and that was awful. At that moment, I would not have described the season as "pure joy." As they gathered themselves together one last time, the only song in my heart was a dirge.

But then a remarkable thing happened. All 26 boys put their arms around each other. They trudged across the wide Willow Brook Park field, then turned around and came all the way back in that same hauntingly wonderful manner: arm in arm, shoulder to shoulder, supporting each other through tears and sorrow, just as they had been there for each other every step of the way all fall.

The healing had begun.

It continued in a post-game huddle. Still physically close, they talked about the season just ended. Player after player described what a great year it had been. They thanked their teammates for showing such passion, poise and skill. The starters praised the reserves for working hard in training to help everyone improve; the nine underclassmen told the 17 seniors they'd learned what it means to commit to a goal, work hard to achieve it, include everyone in the effort, and have a hell of a lot of fun in the process. There were more tears, but already a few smiles snuck through.

It's hard to keep teenagers down for long – even after our intense events of the previous three months fell short of what we wanted – and by the time the bus reached Westport, the Staples soccer team started to understand how much they'd accomplished.

It was nearly midnight; of course they headed to the diner. As they walked in, a few dozen teenagers – riders of the fan bus, who had followed them to New Britain just as they'd followed the team all year long – stood and applauded. It was a classy finish for a classy team, and it provided one more bit of proof that this year's season was a true community event.

The Staples boys soccer program has always prided itself on its family feeling. That sense was enhanced on a glorious October Saturday morning when, after months of work, we dedicated our new terraced seating. Several hundred fans – including former players, former players' parents, and Westport Soccer Association youngsters who will one day play for Staples – packed the hillside to watch the Wreckers win.

As the season gained steam, Staples gathered fans. While the squad rolled to the final match, the players realized they were part of something larger. They were the latest link in a 50-year chain, and they reveled in the feeling.

Teenagers are often accused of caring only for themselves, living just for the moment, but that soccer team understood where they came from, and what will follow them. Every day, we read emails from alumni who felt connected to this squad. Each used different words, but the messages were the same: "We've been there. We know what it's like to form bonds like brothers, and battle each day together. We want you to have the same experience. Cherish it, because the season is short. But the lessons and the feelings last a lifetime."

They understood, too, that they were role models for younger players – after all, the current athletes once sat on the same soccer hill and dreamed of the day they would wear the Staples "S." They signed a few autographs, kicked around with elementary and middle school kids, and smiled as they realized that, several years later, a new generation of soccer players would recall their team's spectacular goals, blazing speed and gravity-defying saves.

Because Staples soccer players love the game and the program – and play in summer pickup matches, winter alumni games and whenever else they can – they know many of the guys who came before them. As alums themselves, they meet the current crop of players. The family grows, year after year. Every family tells legendary tales, of course, and I am delighted that for soccer generations to come, the 2006 team will be the stuff of legend.

I am delighted not because they reached the state finals – though that is a worthy accomplishment – but because of the way they did it. They faced tremendous adversity on the field, though that is true of nearly any team in every sport.

There were also off-the-field issues – matters, literally, of life and death. In early October the father of a popular junior varsity player died, after a year-long struggle with cancer. That Friday morning, varsity players joined the JV at the funeral. For many, it was their first experience with death. A couple of hours later, as the varsity headed down the hill for training, I realized we needed to talk.

I asked what they thought of the service. Most were impressed by the poise of the JV player who eulogized his dad. They were amazed that funny stories were told, light-hearted slides were shown, and that at moments like this there could be equal amounts of laughter and tears.

Death is a part of life, they realized. Before they stretched out and warmed up, I said these final words: "Go home. Tell your parents you love them, and thank them for all they've done for you. You never know when you'll lose someone."

Forty-eight hours later – that Sunday afternoon –an acquaintance called. "One of your players just lost his dad," he said. I thought he meant the JV boy. Instead he delivered the almost surreal news that the father of a varsity player, Neil – the first reserve off the bench, in fact – had just dropped dead of a massive heart attack.

The next morning, I went to the house. Grief hung in the air, as dark as the autumn morning itself was light. Neil, his mother and younger sister, various relatives – all struggled to speak.

But Neil found his voice, and asked: "Can I play this afternoon?" In less than six hours, we had a match.

Of course, I said. And if, at 3:30, you decide you don't want to, that's fine too. In a situation like this, there is no right or wrong answer.

Neil played. He was, as usual, the first player off the bench. And, in a story even a Lifetime movie could not script, he scored three goals and added an assist in a cathartic 8-1 victory. There were tears on the field before, during and after the game; they were mirrored on the hill, where Neil's mother, sister and many relatives were embraced by their other family: our soccer parents and friends.

That same week, a starter's father was hospitalized with what turned out to be terminal cancer. (He died before Christmas, three weeks after our season-ending banquet.) Yet being surrounded by so much misery brought out the best in our boys. They bonded together more strongly than any team I'd seen in three decades of coaching. They were not afraid to speak of death or fear; they were unashamed to cry.

Their tightness was expressed physically, too. One night before an important post-season match, they ate dinner at a player's house and headed upstairs for a team meeting. I walked in last. Though the room was large I saw them huddled together, as if protecting themselves from a storm. As many as possible crammed onto a couple of couches and chairs. A few sat on the arms of the furniture, or scrunched on the floor leaning back into their teammates' legs. One or two sat, completely unselfconsciously, on others' laps.

I was supposed to give a motivational speech, but I did not have to say a word. The next day's game was already won.

Of course, so much emotion proved more than some boys could handle. For one player in particular – a younger varsity player, who had a great future but that year saw relatively little action – the tragedies dredged up the death of his own father two years earlier. The older boys understood Reed had a lot to deal with, and they reached out to him as only adolescents can: with a friendly jab in the shoulder, an invitation to join their pre-game kick-arounds, the offer of a ride home.

I knew he was touched by their care and concern, but I had no idea how much it meant until weeks later, when the final, golden-goal championship match was suddenly over. After the initial stunned heartache subsided; after the team took that now-legendary arm-in-arm walk across the field, and the players stood in a circle and described how much the season had meant to them; after the stadium lights were turned off, we gathered our gear, and headed to the bus for our final ride home.

Suddenly I saw Reed alone by the fence. He sobbed uncontrollably. I asked what was wrong, but he could not answer. His body was wracked by loud, guttural noises. I had never before witnessed such grief; it was as if he had retreated into himself, to a place no one could penetrate.

I put my arm around him. It's okay, I said. We're here for you. We want to help. Just tell us what's wrong.

For 15 minutes, Reed could not speak. Finally, in between heaves of sadness, he explained: It was his fault we lost. He had not worked hard enough in training. If only he had tried harder, the starters would have improved more, and we would have won.

For the first time that night, I cried. How could you not love a team that loved each other so much?

Even more went on that autumn, some of it too personal to recount here – just as the in jokes, the rituals, the special feelings and relationships must remain unwritten. A sports team works hard to succeed; its success or failure – the final score -- is duly noted, and long remembered. But true success cannot be measured so easily. Success lies within each member; at the same time it transcends individual boundaries, and binds everyone together. And though the group eventually breaks up – the season ends; players graduate; some remain close, others fade away -- the memories remain forever.

The memories I have of that soccer season are of pure, unbridled joy. And that is why, in sports, results are measured not only by trophies. In the game of life, the boys of the 2006 Staples High School squad are truly my champions.

IT'S ALL ABOUT PROBLEM-SOLVING

In the 1990s I did something most coaches only dream about: I banned parents from all overseas trips.

This was not a decision made out of malice – okay, that was only one reason. It was certainly not done for the sake of convenience, although a major unintended result was much greater control of the group. I'd much be the ringleader of a zoo, as I was with the players, than a herder of cats, which occurred when parents tagged along.

I decided to leave parents home because, ultimately, a European soccer excursion is a trip for kids. Traveling overseas offers so many benefits beyond the game itself. Dozens of times each day, youngsters face new and unforeseen situations. They are forced to exchange money, then budget it using mathematical skills they never thought necessary (the introduction of the euro took some of the fun away; switching from francs to guilders to deutsche marks could be daunting). They must order food from menus they can't read (and then figure out whether mayonnaise on french fries is culinary progress or not), ride transportation they've never seen ("Dan, what exactly is a trolley?"), settle in with families vastly different from their own (two players stunned the rest of our team as they described sharing an enormous bed with the host family's two sons, father and grandfather), haul their own bags everywhere ("Now do you see why I said to pack lightly?"), and take showers with nozzles held in one hand (parents would not be much help there).

Parents are genetically programmed to leap in wherever they can – and many places they can't – to make things easier for their offspring. When Mom and Dad accompany Dylan and Brittany to Europe, they (the adults) offer to exchange money, then carry it. They take charge of meals, commandeer (and pay for) taxis, bring kids back to the hotel "to relax a bit." And when the child forgets his soccer shoes, parents race off to buy a new pair.

None of that helps youngsters gain maturity, independence or self-confidence. In fact, it's likely to keep them immature, dependent and unconfident. So a while ago I started telling parents: "If you want to go to Europe, great. Enjoy your vacation. It just won't be with us."

That did not make me the most popular youth soccer coach around. It did, however, make our trips even more enjoyable than they had been. And, most importantly, it allowed our players to get even more out of them.

I developed a mantra. Each trip I repeated the same refrain to the players: "It's all about problem-solving." I said it each fall, when we began planning our itinerary. I told it to them during the winter when they raised funds, and in the spring when we trained. All along they nodded politely, humoring me, but they never really understood.

Until they landed overseas. Then – instantly -- they got it.

My assistant coach and I continually told the players, "We'll help you with big problems. If you ever need major assistance, come to us – that's why we're here. But you're soccer players. You're 15 and 16 -- old enough to go to Europe on your own. So we expect you to solve the little problems on your own. Remember, it's all about problem-solving." It got to the point where I said "It's all about problem-solving" more often than "Shoot the ball!" "Get back on defense!" and "Can you please turn down your music so I don't have to listen to that crap?"

My teams do not have many rules. I believe the more things you tell a teenager not to do, the more often he'll try to do them. Rules impose an authoritarian, us-against-them dynamic, the exact antithesis of what a good soccer team needs. And for every rule that is imposed, there must be consequences for breaking it. A coach with a lot of rules can spend so much time trying to enforce them that he has no time for a stroll around the piazza.

But there must be some rules, and the ones we have we expect to be followed. One of the most important is punctuality. This teaches personal responsibility. It teaches team responsibility too, because everyone looks out for each other. Besides, I hate waiting.

Invariably, what happens is this: On our first full day in Europe we orient the players, then get ready to turn them loose. (I choose a small or mid-size city as our initial destination, for a very specific reason. I may be open-minded, but I am not dumb enough to head directly to Amsterdam and say, "Okay, boys, here you go. The Anne Frank House is that way, the Van Gogh Museum is there, and the red light district is just down the street. Enjoy yourselves!")

My assistant coach and I take them to a bus or trolley stop. We explain how to read the schedule. It may not be written in English, but important details like times and days of the week are easy to figure out. We stress the importance of knowing the numbers of buses and trolleys, as well as stops. We tell the players to keep their eyes open for landmarks, and know exactly where they are headed in case they get lost. And then we say, "Be back no later than 5 p.m. See ya!"

"You're not going with us?" they ask, panic-stricken. Suddenly these swaggering boys – who for months have been bragging about how free they will suddenly be – would give anything to have us by their side.

"Nope," we say. "We'll just hang out here for awhile. Don't worry, we won't miss you!"

And like a pack of sheep, they climb on board and head off. All 15 boys cling together – the coolest and the least socially adept; the smartest and the ones with no common sense; the best players and the reserves. For the first time ever, each needs the support of all the others. On that very first bus or trolley ride, new friendships start to form. The entire team begins to bond more strongly. It is an organic process, one that is invisible to the eye and almost impossible to describe. But it always happens, and it always begins that first day, in that first way.

I am never sure where the players end up, though snippets of information float back to me. I do know that most of the time they do not split up at all; if they do, it is into two large groups. In the unfamiliar of streets of Europe – the same streets they fantasized about for so long – there is strength in numbers.

Sometimes they wander around, gawking at the beauty of a place that thrived centuries before the first Europeans landed on our own continent. Sometimes they go to sports stores or (craving familiarity after one full day away) McDonald's. Sometimes they go to sex stores or bars -- and sometimes they amaze themselves by not getting tossed out. (I should say here that I do not endorse those activities. But I do know, from everything I have seen and heard, that sex stores and bars are two places in Europe where virtually every American teenager ends up. It does not matter if you are taking a soccer team from Connecticut or a church group from Mississippi; any youth leader who thinks his kids will not seek these places out is not living on planet Earth.)

Soon – far earlier than they need to, because on the first day they are petrified of being late – the group heads back. They find the bus or trolley stop where they got off. They congratulate themselves for not getting lost. When the bus or trolley arrives, they clamber on board.

And, all together, they head out in the wrong direction.

Because of course my assistant and I have, quite deliberately, not told them that the stop they must gather at to return is *across the street* from the one where they got off. It's not brain surgery, obviously, but to suburban boys who think all buses are yellow and travel only between their driveway and school, it's something they never considered.

So what happens, year after year, is that they return the opposite direction of where they want to go. They are busy chattering, comparing notes and planning their next excursion, when suddenly someone notices what's happening. Invariably the brightest, most alert teammate – and that usually means one more adept at Scrabble than soccer –is the first one on this ball. He analyzes the problem, makes sure everyone gets off as soon as possible, then herds them across the road to the proper bus or trolley stop.

I know all this because it is the first topic of conversation when the group arrives back at our meeting spot. They come with five minutes to spare – not 20 as they'd planned, because of the mix-up – but they fall all over themselves describing their "adventure." They laugh now, more with relief than humor, and effusively praise the player who "saved" them. Suddenly the brainy boy is welcomed into the inner circle. The shared experience tightens all bonds even further. And a very important lesson has been learned.

"So, was there a problem?" I ask.

"Yeah!" they answer in unison.

"And did you solve it?"

"Of course!"

I move in for the kill. "Now you know what we mean when we say, 'It's all about problem-solving.'"

Finally, they get it. They understand that, even though they are just 15 or 16, they have the ability to solve problems on their own. But they understand too that it is far easier to solve them when they work together.

Sometimes, of course, circumstances demand that problem-solving occurs on an individual level. That's what happened the now-legendary night Duke missed the bus in Gothenburg.

He was one of the most marginal players (in terms of soccer talent) I've taken on a trip. He was also one of the brightest (as in the ability to solve complex mathematic equations, or use principles of physics to explain why roller coasters don't drop off their tracks when they turn upside down). Finally, Duke was also one of the most scatter-brained boys I've ever seen (as in his complete inability to be wherever he was supposed to be, whenever he was supposed to be there). That's a challenging combination of traits.

The team was in Gothenburg, Sweden, and the massive Gothia Cup tournament was underway. Over 15,000 players from around the world descend on this charming port city, for a week of soccer and whatever else 15,000 teenagers do in a charming port city (or anywhere else, for that matter). There are games all day, every day, everywhere; then in the evening all 15,000 teenagers converge on Liseberg, an enormous amusement part in the center of this charming port city. There are rides, games, restaurants, an enormous disco – all in an environment so Swedish-safe, it makes Disney World look like "Blade Runner"'s post-apocalyptic L.A.

We were staying in a school a few miles outside the city center. Several dozen teams bunked there, each in its own classroom (this being Sweden, guys and girls teams shared hallways, bathrooms and just about everything else). The name of the school was something like Utomjustenspeciellsommarveckautom, which is pronounced just as it looks but has many more umlauts and circles over vowels that cannot be reproduced here. Because everyone except the player with the hacking cough had a tough time saying it, we just called it "the school." We told the players to make sure they carried the name around with them in case they got lost, which two or three of them might actually have done. Fortunately there were never any communication problems, because one of the many laws in Sweden is that every Swede must speak better English than every American. Furthermore, a trolley line ran right to the school ("right to" in Sweden means half a mile away, but our players quickly learned that such a hike was a small price to pay for many evenings of freedom).

My assistant coach and I knew our players cherished that freedom, and the entire team worked together to maintain it. It was understood that we would give the boys as much freedom as they could handle. If they proved to be responsible, they got more; if they were irresponsible, they got less. And this was indeed a team deal. If one of them screwed up, all the rest might pay. The Three Musketeers had nothing on Westport.

We used the classroom clock as Official Curfew Time. That way, no one could protest, "But my watch said..." The clock was big, too, so there were no excuses about reading it wrong.

For several nights the system worked perfectly. Curfew was midnight, and between 11:30 and 11:50 most of the players streamed in. They made phone calls, ate (they were of course starving, since they had not refueled in at least an hour), and swapped tales (some might even have been true). There was no need to worry; they respected curfew, or at least each other.

But one night at quarter to midnight a group of players rushed in, breathless. They'd caught the last trolley, run all the way from the school stop, and had a story to tell: As they got on at Liseberg, they saw Duke in the distance. He had never been the fastest player; bad blisters now slowed him further. The trolley left without him.

As both hands of the clock neared 12, Duke was nowhere to be seen. The boys' laughter at his predicament turned to worry. What was I going to do? Would it affect them? And how the heck was Duke ever going to find his way home along the dark, winding streets, all with names even longer and less familiar than the school's?

Outwardly, I projected serenity. Don't worry, I said. Nothing will happen until he is officially late. He's still got, um, three minutes. Inside, of course, my mind was churning. What would I do? Should I punish Duke alone, and if so, how? Was it wrong for his teammates to leave after they saw him? Then again, it *was* the last trolley of the night – and Duke was the one who had not reached it on time. All along, I worried: Is Duke okay? What happens if he never comes back? I wondered if I might be coaching my very last overseas team.

It took two and a half minutes to think through all that. The clock edged closer to midnight. Finally, at 11:59:30 – with, literally, 30 seconds remaining before curfew – Duke burst through the door.

Some people seldom sweat, and Duke was one of them. Furthermore, because he didn't play a lot, he had few occasions to over-exert himself. But that night sweat poured from every pore of his body. And remember, this was Sweden; there was a midnight sun, sure, but we're still talking reindeer and tundra.

Instinctively, Duke looked up at the clock. By now a few seconds had passed, so he was maybe 20 seconds ahead of curfew. When he realized he had made it – and given new meaning to the term "with seconds to spare" – he broke into an enormous grin. You'd have thought he had just scored the winning goal at the Gothia Cup (or, more likely with Duke, won the Nobel Prize in Physics). His teammates, meanwhile – relieved to see him, and equally delighted that their curfew-dependent leash would not be tightened – mobbed him in game-winning fashion.

After expressing their delight, everyone wanted to know: What happened?

"I missed the last trolley," Duke said.

"So what did you do?" we clamored.

"I ran," he said. "What else was I supposed to do?"

Every boy, and both coaches, instantly pictured Duke – gangly, slow, blister-burdened Duke – lumbering up the hills of Gothenburg, from the amusement park all the way to our school. It was at least four miles; the twists and turns were innumerable.

One boy voiced the question we all were thinking: "How the hell did you know where to go?"

Duke looked around the room. He gave each of us a look that said we were a village of idiots, and in tones reserved for *v-e-r-y* slow children explained: "I followed the trolley tracks!"

There was a pause, while his words sunk in. The solution was so simple, so clear – and so likely to be missed, in a moment of pressure, by the rest of us. No one knew what to say.

Finally one boy broke the silence. "He followed the trolley tracks! That's amazing! Duke, you are a fucking genius."

But Duke – by now basking in new adulation, the most unlikely hero of the long day – had the last word.

"Hey, Dan," he said, tossing my mantra right back at me. "It was easy.

He paused. "It's all about problem solving."

DEATH COMES QUICKLY

There can be no worse experience for a youth coach than an athlete dying young. Automobile accidents, freak injuries, cancer – all take their toll, all too soon. Somehow, though, the loss seems even crueler when a teenager dies by his own hand. Suicide, the saying goes, is a permanent solution to a temporary problem. For the survivors, the pain lasts forever.

Bill was born in 1970. In 1985 he asphyxiated himself, in the garage of his house. He was 15 years old. He has now been dead longer than he was alive.

Bill's friends and teammates are already adults. They have scattered around the world, doing adult things. They are being promoted, forming their own companies, being downsized, practicing medicine and law, getting married, having children, getting divorced, suffering midlife crises, buying and losing houses, battling alcoholism, becoming full participants in their communities.

Bill will always be 15.

I think about him every March 14 – his birthday. I think about him every June 18 – that's the day he died. I think about him many other days, too. I was his coach, after all; we shared a fun time together. Besides, apart from his family and nearly everyone in Westport, who else will remember him? Fifteen years is not enough time to make one's mark on the world. But Bill surely tried.

I knew him only a short while – one season, in the fall of his freshman year in high school – but he touched me deeply. Bill touched everyone he met. He had an engaging personality, a winning smile, a way of reaching your soul with just a word or glance. He had a school full of friends, a town full of admirers. Soccer was just a small part of his life; he was also a golfer, dancer, partier, jogger, busboy, Key Club member, foundation digger, camper, Spanish honors student and confidant. His teachers, employers, the parents of guy friends and girlfriends – no one who knew Bill remained unaffected.

Bill certainly touched me. The first time I met him was the end of summer, just before school began. He came out for the freshman team. I liked what I saw – his speed, his potential, his attitude – but after a few days he disappeared.

When I called to ask if he was still interested in trying out, he sounded uncertain. "I don't know. I don't think I'm good enough," he said.

I was stunned. I was used to telling boys who believed they were fantastic that they were really not as good as they thought. Here was a player who *was* good enough, yet had no idea.

I told him I would be the judge; I wanted him to play, and he would make the team. That made us both happy. It was the first time I realized Bill was a special person, so different from the thick-skinned athletes I was used to working with. His sensitivity lurked so close to the surface.

Bill returned the next day, and the other players were as happy to see him as I. He brought joy to us all, though no one could figure out how someone with such skinny, bowed legs could be so quick.

Bill stuck with soccer, with what I soon discovered was typical determination and enthusiasm. He had an immense, genuine desire to learn and improve. He asked plenty of questions: "Did I make the right play? Why aren't my passes going where I want them? What do I need to work on to improve?" Refreshingly, he actually wanted to know the answers. He did not act like many other players, who ask only what they think the coach hopes to hear. (An English teacher noticed the same thing, and showed me a paper he had written on the importance of being a good role model for his younger brother. "You know, he really means it," she said with amazement.)

As the soccer season progressed, so did Bill. He worked his way up, methodically but steadily, to where he was an early sub (on a team of 27 – what was I thinking back then?!). The highlight came late in the year. He won the ball deep in the backfield, turned on his jets and, using the dribbling skills and strategic sense he'd worked on all fall, raced up the sideline to deliver a great, long cross into the goalmouth. A teammate headed the ball in for a goal. It was one of the prettiest plays of the season, and I still remember the entire team racing over to congratulate a grinning #25.

As the school year wore on Bill continued to impress his teachers, fellow ninth graders, even upperclassmen. (And upperclasswomen: Nearly every girl had a crush on the cute ninth grader with the million-dollar smile.) His hangout was the library. He studied, but also used it as a social center. Students were not supposed to talk there, but Bill communicated with a grin, a note, or simply by sitting at a table with someone who looked lonely.

I talked a fair amount with Bill that year, even after soccer ended. It's easy to walk right by someone at Staples High School, even with no one else around. In a crowded hallway, conversation is impossible. But Bill always said hi.

Our conversations were usually about positive topics: his work, friends, school, my latest trip. The last time we talked was the morning of the day he died. Final exams had just started. I asked about summer plans. "I'm getting a job," he said.

"Does it have a name?" I wondered.

"I'm not sure yet," he said. "I've got a couple of leads."

"Excellent," I said. "Let me know. If I don't see you, have a great summer. See you later."

"Thanks a lot, Dan," Bill said. "You too. See ya."

Six hours later, he killed himself.

Today, whenever I meet Bill's friends, the conversation always turns back to him. We remember his life. We wonder where he would be now, and what he would be doing. We rue the senselessness of his death. Nearly three decades later, the pain of his passing remains strong.

There is, however, one difference. Years ago, we felt sad that Bill died. Today we are mad.

Bill is remembered in more than chance conversations. From time to time, I see telltale signs on his grave. His bones lie in a gentle cemetery less than a mile from the home where he lived and died. Once or twice a year, I stop by. I prefer going on my bike, in the warm sun, but occasionally I drive there in the rain or mist. More often than not I find something on his headstone – flowers, a trinket, an arrangement of rocks. They send a message to Bill, and to the rest of us who still live: *We remember*.

In life, Bill brought many people together. In death, he does the same. One day a few years ago, his best friend visited for a couple of days from out West. As always, he headed to Bill's grave. It is peaceful there; a person can reflect on Bill's life, and his own, and come away feeling both serious and serene.

While he was there, a girl from Bill's class – now a grown woman – drove up. She too was visiting her parents in Westport, and she too felt drawn to the cemetery. The two classmates had not seen each other in a decade. They hugged. They cried. They talked about Bill. And as all of us still do, these many years later, they asked each other one question: *Why?*

Whenever I see Bill's cemetery, I recall Thanksgiving weekend the year he died. Driving past, I saw a touch football game taking place on the broad field just inside the entrance. A ball spiraled through the air; outstretched hands grabbed for it, and as one boy outwrestled the others, raced into the "end zone" and was mobbed by teammates, I felt appalled. *Such desecration*, I thought.

Then I got closer, and recognized the players. They were Bill's friends; some had played soccer with him, and for me. Many had stood in that very cemetery five months earlier, dressed uncomfortably in jackets and ties, grappling with raw emotions they had never before felt. Now, goofing around in their jeans and sneakers, they looked much more at ease. They were not out of place at all, I realized. They were simply honoring their friend's memory the best way they knew.

It has been a long time since I have seen a touch football game in that cemetery. Of course, Bill's friends are now over 40 years old. Most no longer live here. Besides, with families, jobs and responsibilities of their own, they do not have much time to play games.

I know, however, that they all remember Bill. And when they return to Westport, they make sure to visit their friend.

In some ways, much has changed since 1985. When I first went to the cemetery, Bill's grave was the freshest. It took a while for the harsh dirt to be replaced with green grass. It was easy to find Bill then: He was buried in the last row, underneath a large tree.

Today I must search harder to find him. There are a dozen rows of newer graves. I am not even sure which tree is Bill's. His spot no longer seems special, in the cemetery scheme of things – although, of course, it is to me.

Yet if much has changed in the cemetery over the intervening years, in other ways nothing has. Bill's grave site is still covered with grass every spring and summer, with leaves each fall, and snow in winter. Bill's name remains engraved in stone. By now I have given up the hope that one day it will not be there, that he will magically live again. His birth date and death date have not changed. They never will.

And each time I say the same silent prayer. I pray for Bill. I pray for his family, friends and teammates. And I pray that never again will I

41

have to visit the grave of a young athlete who, like Bill, felt none of the faith, hopes and dreams that all who knew him shared.

I did not coach Bryan. He moved the year before I began working with his age group. But his suicide – he shot himself in his parents' house – reverberated as powerfully as if he were one of my own. I was coaching his former teammates that spring, and in less than two weeks we were leaving for Europe.

Bryan, like Bill, seemed to have everything in the world. He too was smart, athletic, good-looking and popular; like Bill's, his family truly loved him. Death by his own hand shook his friends to their cores. Each boy asked *Why?* And although no boy asked another question – *If Bryan could do this to himself, what does it say about me?* – the question hung heavily in the air.

By a stunning coincidence, Bryan's funeral was held the morning after Todd became a father. Todd was 17 years old; a few days earlier, he had finished his junior year. He was a responsible boy, but he was also just a boy. He and his girlfriend had plenty of sex, most but not all of it safe, and their fire was so hot they got burned.

She was adamantly opposed to abortion, and Todd faced the situation like a man. He supported her emotionally and -- with his parents' assistance -- financially. A naturally quiet boy, he seldom talked about his predicament with his teammates, and never with me. But I knew what was happening, and watched closely to see how impending fatherhood would impact him and his friends.

I heard about the birth of Todd's son on the way to Bryan's funeral. Sitting in the stifling, filled-to-capacity church, I pinballed through every emotion. I was both happy and petrified for Todd, his girlfriend and his baby; I agonized over Bryan's death, was warmed by the turnout of his

42

friends, and at the same time worried about the depth of their teenage emotions.

After the service, hundreds of mourners filled the church basement to reminisce. It was an intense several hours. I stayed as long as I could, leaving only because I had a practice to run. Europe loomed just a few days away.

The weather was hot, the players who had attended the funeral could not concentrate, and an odd undercurrent ran through the entire team. The younger players did not know about Todd's situation – no one had ever mentioned it – so the older boys were unable to talk about the one thing they wanted to. I cut the training session short, and brought everyone together underneath a tree.

"Guys," I said, "you know we're training for a big trip. We've worked hard all year to get ready for Europe, and it's one of the most important things you'll do in your soccer lives. But sometimes things happen that overshadow soccer. Today is one of those days. Instead of soccer, we're going to talk about life and death."

For the next hour, that's all we did. I told them about Bryan's funeral, and Todd's baby. All had heard about the suicide, but the younger boys were shocked to learn they would travel to Europe with a father around their own age. We discussed the importance of communication: how to talk to loved ones or trusted friends about painful emotions, and how to talk to sexual partners about sex. We discussed too the eternal cycle of life and death. We concluded that we would mourn Bryan, and it was right to feel angry at his senseless death. At the same time, however, we could thrill to the birth of a new human being, and do all we could to help make Todd and his baby's lives happy ones.

When the talk ended, I felt more exhausted than after the most physical training session. Many players gathered their belongings and left quietly – more introspective than I had ever seen them – but a few older ones lingered. They said they had wanted to say something about Todd, but had no idea how to bring it up. They thanked me for treating the subject sensitively – I supposed, with a wince, they thought I'd turn it into a joke, or criticize Todd for being stupid. Then they asked what kind of gift would be good. Clearly, they were navigating new seas, and were grateful they did not have to sail alone.

I felt happy for them, and for Todd too. At the same instant, I realized Bryan would never get a chance to buy anyone a baby present – nor would he ever receive one.

For the first and only time at practice, I cried.

A different type of death – equally sudden, just as random, but if anything even more horrifying – occurred on September 11, 2001. Nearly three thousand people lost their lives that day. Three thousand murdered men and women – all gone, all senselessly, brutally and tragically -- is too enormous a number to comprehend.

So let me tell you about one of them.

Fifteen years ago, Scott was a boy adults loved – and loved to hate. He was a 1980's version of Huck Finn: adventurous, fun-loving, anti-authority and sharp as cheddar cheese. He was clever, witty, and possessed of a remarkable ability to push every envelope further than it had ever been designed to bulge. Even more amazingly, Scott knew just when to stop pushing, so the envelope never ripped.

For four years I was Scott's soccer coach. Our first team was the Warriors, a Westport Soccer Association-sponsored team back in the day when travel soccer was as far as players could go. We went pretty far, all the way to the Eastern U.S. regional tournament, plus a summer tour of Europe. I also coached Scott when he joined the Staples High

School freshman team. Those four years spanned ages 12 to 16. Anyone who knows an adolescent, or has been one himself, realizes those are not the easiest years for even the most level-headed youngster. And no one – including Scott's dozens of closest friends -- would describe him as level-headed.

Which may be one reason why, in between bouts of going crazy over his antics, I joined the long list of people charmed by him.

Two stories capture his essence perfectly. Europe was the scene for both. Scott and his teammates were 15 years old.

We were in transit from Sweden. We had traveled by bus for a while, and stopped in Denmark for dinner before catching a train for the long ride to Luxembourg. We left the restaurant for a quick walk to the station. Time was short; so was my patience. Teenagers don't care about clocks, but trains do.

Suddenly someone said, "Dan, where's Scott?" I took a quick count; he was indeed missing.

I was furious. He had broken so many rules: He had wandered off alone, not told us where he was going, and put the entire group in jeopardy.

As we broke into small search parties, one boy asked, "What are you gonna do?"

I wanted the players to realize how angry I was. "We'll leave without him!" I thundered. "He probably doesn't even know what country he's in!" I would not have abandoned him, of course – at least, I don't think I would have – but my harsh words galvanized the troops to search even harder for Scott than they already planned.

Ten minutes later he rounded the corner. Scott's face was ashen; he knew he'd messed up big-time. I was more relieved than anyone, but as the players hugged him and peppered him with questions (it turns out that as we left the restaurant he went to the bathroom), I maintained my coach's face.

"Scott," I said sharply. "Do you know what country you're in?"

His eyes grew wide. He knew this was an important question, one he absolutely had to get right. He thought long and hard. I thought I could see his brain synapses firing.

He looked at me earnestly. "Copenhagen?" he asked.

"That's good enough," I said. And, against my best judgment, I smiled. No one could stay mad at Scott for long.

Just a few hours later, we settled into our train compartments. Night had fallen, but for the boys a new adventure was about to begin. My main worry was that they might be too loud for the other passengers, yet as I passed Scott's berth I had a new fear. The window was wide open, and Scott's head and upper body leaned all the way outside. He wanted an up-close-and-personal view of the German countryside, and he was getting it.

I raced in, yanking his body back. I asked what he was doing, using words I am sure had never been heard on a German train. Scott stared at me blankly.

I drove my point home. "Look!" I yelled, pointing to the warning signs against putting one's head out the window. They were plastered throughout the rail car, in six different languages; each had a little pictograph, showing a stylized head far out a window, with the universally recognized red slash running through it. Unfortunately, not one of those languages was English.

"How am I supposed to know what they say?" Scott asked. He knew he was wrong; he knew I knew he was wrong; he also knew he was the only one on the team who could say that, and get away with it. I tried not to laugh. I did not succeed.

I thought of those two stories on September 11. I heard the devastating news that Scott worked with his brother Keith at Cantor Fitzgerald; both their offices were on the 104th floor of the World Trade Center. They, and more than 600 of their colleagues, never had a chance.

After leaving Staples for private school, Scott had gone on to Colgate University. He settled down a bit, turning his quick, incisive mind away from mischief and toward the business world. Before Cantor Fitzgerald, he worked for HBO. Business was a natural field for someone with such strong people skills. He grew up, but retained his adventurous ways. He grew older, but his spirit never faded. Now, because of the unfathomable acts of a few madmen, Scott would never get a chance to grow old.

As news about Scott spread, his friends gathered in New York. I was there in spirit; my first obligation was to be in Westport, with the high school soccer team where I was assistant coach. But I could not stop thinking about Scott; I could not get his mischievous teenage face out of my mind. So it was natural that, when someone asked if I agreed with our school's decision to play the opening game of the season as scheduled, just two days after the terrorist attack, my thoughts turned to Scott.

There was no right or wrong response to that question, yet my answer was firm. I answered that a young man I had once coached had just been killed, and his friends were honoring his memory by remembering all the great times they shared through the years. They were talking about games won and lost, and everything they did together off the field as well (though I knew many of Scott's escapades, I am sure some of those tales would be news to me). Scott's friends, I said, were not spending those hours recalling algebra classes or social studies tests. What bonded them so closely during those crucial adolescent years – and what drew them together once again, during such an unspeakably grim event -- was the time they spent as young soccer players training, playing, running, laughing and, of course, plotting behind the coach's back.

So yes, I said, the high school soccer season should begin as scheduled. It was time for the 2001 Staples athletes to begin forming their own bonds, making their own memories, strengthening their own lives. In fact, they had to play. There was not a moment to waste.

The friendships teenagers develop on athletic fields can last a lifetime. How devastatingly sad that Scott's lifetime was so short. Yet how joyful I am that I shared a small part of his with him.

And then there was Preston.

The 2006 fall season was the most intense I have ever experienced as a coach. So much happened on our run to the state finals. There were two incredible penalty kick victories; a wild, golden-goal final match – and, along the way, the deaths and terminal illnesses of several fathers of players. (You have probably read about it already, in the chapter "They Are the Champions.")

Throughout that amazing autumn, Preston was the glue that kept our Staples High School team together. His passionate play on the field ensured that no one slacked off. He did not care who you were; he demanded the best from everyone. When you saw Preston, drenched in sweat on the coldest November night, you raised your game. Even the lowliest bench-sitter was inspired by Preston. Seeing the fire in his eyes, reserves cheered even harder, willing their teammates on.

Off the field, he was a unifying force. He was closer to some teammates than others, sure. But he made time for everyone, and in the darkest hours – the days of funerals and tears – Preston made sure, with a quick smile glance, that his teammates knew he cared.

In the summers that followed, long after graduation, the '06 team stayed almost scarily tight. They hung together each night. They played soccer incessantly, ripping through the high school and alumni teams in our Watermelon Cup 6-v-6 league. They set the standard for "teamness" and dedication, providing perfect role models for up-and-coming athletes. And the most stalwart player of all was Preston. The only time, in fact, he did not play, or help younger players improve their game, was when he was in Ghana, serving on a soccer-related service project.

On August 18, 2009 – the first day of pre-season practice at the University of Mary Washington – Preston collapsed. A freshman player performed CPR. His best friend since kindergarten in Westport; his former Staples and current Mary Washington teammate, held his hand.

It was no use. Preston died on his beloved soccer field, the victim of an enlarged heart.

To the 2006 squad – some of whom heard the news while, typically, playing soccer in Westport before leaving for college – this was the cruelest blow of all. The heart of their team had been ripped from them. He'd been betrayed by his own heart.

They were not the only young men devastated. Mary Washington players had just watched their friend and teammate die. I cannot conceive of a horror like that.

Westport rallied quickly, as it often does. Matt's mother offered to host the 25 Mary Washington players who came north from Virginia. Twenty-five mattresses were found. Food was donated; transportation arranged.

Three nights after Preston died, a candlelight service was held on the terrace at the top of our field. Preston's high school and college teammates spoke movingly, and eloquently, about what he had meant to them.

I announced that his #15 jersey would not be retired; instead it will be worn by a player whose passion, intensity and talent is worthy of Preston. And, at the end of each season, the player who earned #15 will tell me who is most worthy of wearing it the following year.

Then, everyone turned around. At the base of the hill – just off the sideline near midfield – "15" was lit by candles. They burned brightly – burned with a fervor that Preston always had. For many long minutes high school and college players, parents, alumni, young kids and family members sat on our granite benches, and watched the candles burn. No one said a word. No one had to.

The following afternoon, a service was held in a church in the woods. This time, words said everything. Preston's parents spoke; so did relatives, teammates, coaches, and his ever-present wingman, Matt. All painted a portrait of a remarkable young man.

But the most moving words were Preston's own. His father read Preston's speech from December 2006. It was his senior banquet. He was not a captain, but he asked if he could say something. I had no idea what it would be, but I did not hesitate. Preston, I knew, would give it to all of us straight.

That night, his words moved many parents to tears. Less than three years later, they once again drew tears, this time for several hundred mourners. But through our tears, we smiled. Through his father's voice, we heard Preston speak once again. And through his words, we realized that thanks to his spirit, he could never really die.

Preston said:

"At the beginning of the year I would never have seen any of this happening to us. I wasn't surprised that we did as well as we did; it was more about the fashion we did it in.

"I also never thought that I would exit this last year in a Staples High School jersey as such a changed person, but sometimes the best changes and best experiences are unforeseen.

"So many people use soccer and sports as a metaphor for life, but no team has made it truer than this one. It wasn't just games that were won, life-long relationships were forged, memories were made, and life lessons have been learned.

"Most importantly this team has inspired everyone involved with it. I have been inspired by my teammates to become a better teammate, friend, brother, son, and most importantly a better person. I was also inspired by their passion. They not only had so much passion for the game of soccer, they also had a passion for each other, truly like brothers.

"These bonds, filled with care, were ones that were built on time, dependent on trust, tested under the fire of competition and strengthened with the common love of the game. The only way that I can explain this bond to you is that when we huddle up I can look every one of my teammates in the eye and I know that they will do everything they can for me, and I hope that they know that I would do anything for them.

"I never knew the true power of our friendships until tragedy struck midway through the year. It would be easy for a team to crumble under such adversity, but we rose up hand in hand, and although it wasn't the true start to our season, that's when we had meaning to our season. From then on we walked together, sat together, ate together, and hung out together.

"When our season finally ended, we left the field just as when we started our mission, hand in hand. It was at this point when I appreciated all the experiences from this season because these were life lessons I couldn't have learned anywhere else. I believe that the life lessons I have learned from playing with these incredibly special people have made me into a better person.

"Most importantly my journey in the last two years have taught me that no matter what life hands to you, and more importantly how it is handed to you, the only thing you can do is keep on moving. So that's what we are doing here. We are moving forward, some are going to college, some aren't, some know what they are going to do, some don't, but no matter where you are moving on to I beg you never to forget this Staples team and the passion that we not only played soccer with, but the passion we lived life with.

"Some teams are meant for greatness but this team was meant to live on forever in our minds and our hearts, and to take a line from Friday Night Lights: 'Boys, my heart is full. What about yours?'"

A TEENAGER'S DREAM

And then there was the coed sleepover.

Things were going well during the Staples High School season. Nearly 10 games into the regular season, we were undefeated. We had let in only two goals. Now we were getting ready for our only non-league match of the fall, at Brookfield. I'd scheduled this the previous year as a way to play a quality opponent (for experience), yet hopefully pick up a win (for state tournament seedings, which are based solely on season record).

As soon as I got to the high school, I knew something was up. Players gathered in clusters, talking furtively. They checked text messages with more than their usual urgency, something I'd previously thought impossible. There was an unmistakable frisson in the air, though I had no idea why.

The hour-long bus ride was raucous. Our guys were usually good about focusing, but this time they focused on everything but soccer. I still did not know why that was, but the snippets of conversation floating from the back of the bus to the front had nothing to do with the Wreckers, the Bobcats, or anything remotely close in the wide world of sports.

Our warm-up was desultory. I bull-whipped my captains into getting the players going; my usual task was reining them in from warming up too much. My pre-game speech was out of the I-hope-you're-ready-for-Brookfield-because-they're-sure-ready-for-you book. And I wasn't kidding. The stands were packed. Music pounded. The home team players looked pumped.

My fears proved well-founded. The Bobcats scored a goal two minutes after the opening whistle. They got another two minutes before halftime. It was 3-0 before we managed a face-saving, shutout-averting late score. Still, there was no denying: This was an ass-kicking. Brookfield did to us exactly what we'd done all season long to other teams.

But no one seemed to care.

Our players raced to the bus. Their desire to get out of town was understandable. Their reaction to the lopsided defeat was not. Within minutes, the decibel count – silence would have been appropriate, quiet mourning acceptable – roared back to pre-game levels. I had a hard time hearing, though, because steam was escaping from both ears.

My last words to the team, as we pulled into school that Saturday night near 11 p.m., were: "We've got a big week coming up: games Monday and Wednesday, and undefeated Ridgefield on Friday. Get some rest."

The players had difficulty listening, because they were climbing over each other in their race to get off the bus. They gunned their cars out of the parking lot – and not because they were rushing to go home and sleep.

Nearly 24 hours later – Sunday night – a parent emailed me. "I guess the coed sleepover was not a good idea," the message said.

Coed sleepover?

Sure, the parent replied. You knew about it, right?

Um, no.

In fact, as the story unfolded it became clear there was a reason I had not known about the coed sleepover: There had been an active conspiracy to keep it from me.

The event -- which took place immediately after the Brookfield game, and included players on the boys and girls soccer team – had been organized by the parents of a female player. Just a couple of hours before we boarded the bus, they'd emailed the boys' parents: Tell your sons not to forget their sleeping bags and blankets! No wonder one of them forgot his soccer shoes.

On Monday I talked with the captains, and several players. I learned that part of the reason for the loud voices on the bus ride home was because several players realized a coed sleepover the night after a lopsided loss might not be the best idea. They suggested canceling – or at least postponing – it. Most of their teammates disagreed. A heated debate – though not loud enough for me to hear the actual words – ensued during much of the ride.

Knowing of my displeasure – the steam still billowed from my ears – our guys brought their A-game on Monday. We dispatched of whichever .500 team we were playing pretty easily, and the players gathered around for what they assumed would be my usual platitude-filled post-game speech.

Motioning to our assistant coach, I said: "Kurt and I spent all of yesterday trying to figure out what we did wrong before Brookfield. We went over everything: training sessions, pre-game preparation, personnel, tactics. And you know what? We didn't do anything wrong. You did. You guys had no interest in playing Saturday night. All you cared about was what was going on afterwards. This was Brookfield's Super Bowl – and your pre-game.

"You wasted my entire day, and Kurt's. You owe us a day of our lives back. So we won't train tomorrow. We've got a game Wednesday, but you've got tomorrow off. Do whatever you want. Have another coed sleepover – I don't care. It's clear that whatever we're saying, you're not listening to it. Goodbye -- see you Wednesday."

Then Kurt and I walked away.

The players sat in stunned silence. The thing they'd always wished for – a day off in the middle of the season – was suddenly theirs. They had no idea what to do with it.

They gathered together and (I knew they would) decided to get together on their own. Showing uncommon wisdom, they met on Tuesday not at the high school (where they could have gotten me in trouble for training without supervision), but at an elementary school. According to information I gleaned later, they talked for a long time about how they'd screwed up – not just Saturday night, but at other times during the season. They pointed fingers at teammates, and themselves. They vowed to change.

A determined bunch arrived for Wednesday's match. I could tell things were different when players filled and carried the water jugs down the hill without being reminded multiple times. When they took off their iPods for warm-ups without being told. When, after crushing the other team, they picked up the trash around our bench area, then searched for more tasks to do.

That night I got a call from a father on the girls team. "I hear you're blaming us for the loss to Brookfield," he said.

"That's right," I said. "I am."

"Well, I don't think that's fair," he replied. "The sleepover was after the game. There's no connection at all."

"They're 16-year-old boys," I said. "They can concentrate on only one thing at a time. They can concentrate on soccer, or they can concentrate on what they hope is going to happen after the game. It's pretty clear what they were thinking about."

"Well, nothing bad went on," he countered. "Parents were there the whole time. There was no drinking, no drugs. Everyone stayed in their own sleeping bags. All they did was play basketball and dodgeball all night."

All they did was play basketball and dodgeball all night! The night after playing 80 minutes of soccer, and getting their asses kicked from here to Brookfield, and back!

"So they were up all night, running around playing games," I said. "Even if they slept all day Sunday, when did they do their homework? What did it do to their sleep patterns? And they had a game on Monday – luckily it was against a team that wasn't anywhere near as good as Brookfield."

"What they do on their own time is up to them," the father said. "I don't think you can tell them what to do then. They lost because they didn't play well."

I was not going to convince this otherwise bright and successful man that the reason they didn't play well was because parents had organized a coed sleepover with teenage boys and girls. Our players understood – and that's what counted.

As it turns out (don't tell the father!), the coed sleepover was one of the best things that happened all year. It forced our players to think long and hard about what they'd done – and to realize that my "actions have consequences" mantra was more than mere words. It got them communicating honestly with each other – saying tough words, and listening to them. It led to a laser-like focus for the next several games. We kicked ass.

But – being 16-year-old kids – that focus eventually dimmed. After a successful run through our three-game league tournament (dominating the finals 4-1), we stumbled in round two of the state tourney. Up 2-0 early in the second half against a formidable Newtown side, we let up two goals. Tied 2-2, we recovered our form. But we were thwarted time and again by an excellent keeper. Penalty kicks loomed.

After two rounds of penalties we trailed 2-1. Fortunately, Newtown's third shot clanked off the goalpost; equally fortunately, we made our last three. Their fifth kicker stepped up to the spot, took two steps, and launched his shot into outer space. I think it's still orbiting earth.

Our players celebrated jubilantly. Underneath their jubilation, though, they knew they had dodged a bullet – an entire nuclear weapon, really.

The next day in school several of them said, "We're rattled." I had never heard athletes use that word about themselves; it's what opposing fans use when a player has just done something very uncool or foolish, like putting a penalty kick into orbit. So before training we talked about what had happened.

I told the team they'd just had a near-death experience. This is not really life and death, I emphasized – only high school soccer – but I drew out the analogy. When people survive a near-death experience, they return to their old lives with a new sense of purpose. They see colors more vividly; they tell family members and friends how much they love them; they savor every moment they've been given back to live.

In soccer terms, I said, let's do that. We may have one state tournament match left; ideally, we'll have three. Let's enjoy each second of every game. Let's make the most of whatever opportunities remain. And let's be sure to tell everyone how much we appreciate them.

We kicked ass in the quarterfinals. We outlasted superb, #4-in-the-nation-and-undefeated-to-that-point Glastonbury in the semis, 3-2. (Interestingly, we went up 1-0, were tied 1-1, and climbed back on top 2-1, all in the span of three minutes before halftime. Talk about learning lessons from the previous game!)

The final against New Milford was anticlimactic. On a stunning fall afternoon we scored twice in the first five minutes, then twice right after halftime, to win 4-0. In the 61-year history of the Connecticut state tournament largest schools' division, that was the largest margin of victory. Three thousand spectators thronged Ridgefield's Tiger Hollow, and unless you were a New Milford fan, it was a wonderfully glorious day.

After rushing into the stands to celebrate with our fans, taking several victory laps and posing for dozens of photos, our players made their way to the bus. The trip home took less than an hour, but – sitting together, medals around their necks, passing the state championship plaque back and forth – it was a ride they will never forget.

I sat quietly, thinking about the bus ride from Brookfield a month earlier – ironically, the same route. The talk this time, though just as loud, was different. I was sure the players were reliving every moment of the game, congratulating each other on a tremendous accomplishment – and talking about the post-game party I assumed they'd been planning ever since they knew they'd be in the championship match.

I was wrong. Months later, I learned that the bus ride home was devoted almost entirely to figuring out where and how they would celebrate. "We didn't dare plan anything ahead of time," one of the captains finally explained. "Honestly, Dan, no one said a word about a party until the game was over."

I still don't know many details of that night. Including whether they celebrated with a coed sleepover or not.

HARE KRISHNA

Compared with two decades ago, nearly everything about today's air transportation system is worse. Security lines are longer, the pretzels are smaller, and thanks to the hub-and-spoke system, a cloudburst in Chicago now delays flights nationwide for days.

One element of air travel, however, has happily gone the way of the barf bag: Hare Krishnas. If you are of a certain age – or ever saw the movie "Airplane!" – you remember those saffron robe-wearing, shaved head-sporting, tambourine-thumping banes of airports coast to coast. They were the Internet pop-up ads of yore: unavoidable, persistent, always appearing at the worst possible time. In the space of just a few years, the Hare Krishnas managed to turn one of the world's most oldest, most honored religions into one of the most loathed.

But airports eventually found a way to ban them, freeing up valuable space for Cinnabon stalls and Sunglass Huts. The Hare Krishnas took to the streets, where all good zealots belong. That is where the Westport Warriors found them, one evening in Harvard Square.

Our U-16 team was playing in a tournament in nearby Needham, and Saturday night loomed. The devil makes work for idle hands, especially at hotels filled with 16-year-old girls who just changed out of their soccer jerseys into something far more shapely, so I hustled my boys off to the big city. We ate dinner in Boston's Quincy Market, then crossed the Charles River into Cambridge. I wanted to give my players a taste of street life, Ivy League style; to show them life is far more than soccer balls and soccer girls.

Westport teenagers don't get out of the suburbs much, so the Saturday night scene intrigued them. They wandered in and out of the head shops – I mean, bookstores -- listened to the street musicians, and marveled at drivers even ruder than those in Connecticut.

And then they saw the Hare Krishnas.

There were a dozen or so, chanting and swaying and trolling for money on the sidewalk along Mass Ave. They were rhythmic yet jangly, forceful yet serene. They were also bald.

The suburban boys had no idea what to make of all this. Most had never seen a Hare Krishna, this being the post-airport-ban days, yet a few knew a bit about them. My players, whose religious affiliations ranged all the way from Methodist to Presbyterian (with a few Jews and Catholics thrown in for exotica) talked among themselves, pointing and gesticulating like at a bizarre zoo exhibit. Jerry, a bold and outspoken player who never shied from a crowd, walked over to engage one of the creatures in conversation.

He asked why the Hare Krishna had joined a cult. He wondered what the Krishna's parents thought. And then, smirking, he demanded to know if the Hare Krishna was celibate. The Krishna struggled to explain, but Jerry pounded away.

His tone was aggressive, challenging, superior – and thoroughly obnoxious. He relished the debate, not because he was listening to the answers, but because the entire team had gathered around, egging him on. The sandal was now on the other foot.

I stepped up, interrupting Jerry's questions. "So," I asked the Krishna. "Do you know Greg Willman?"

The Krishna looked startled, but suddenly a smile spread across his face. "Yes," he said, speaking in a stilted yet endearing way. "In fact, I am right now wearing his robe."

Suddenly the attention shifted to me. "Dan, you know this dude?" Jerry asked.

No, I responded. But I knew Greg. In fact, I had coached him, just a few years earlier. He was one of the best players I ever had, I said: Tall, athletic, graceful, as smooth a player as you could want. I took Greg to tournaments just like this one, and we wouldn't have won without him. In fact, I said – I couldn't resist – I wish I had him now. He'd take your spot for sure, Jerry.

Instantly the players forgot the Hare Krishna; they aimed their questions at me. Is Greg really a Hare Krishna? When did he join? Why? Did he have to stop playing soccer? What do his parents think?

Greg was just like you guys, I explained. He was a popular kid, and a great skier too. But school didn't work for him; he got into drugs and alcohol, and his parents shipped him off to private school. I lost track of him for a while, but heard he joined the Hare Krishnas. He cleaned up his act, apparently. And while his parents weren't exactly thrilled that Greg traded a soccer ball for a swami, they realized the Hare Krishnas gave him things he hadn't before: a bit of structure, and ideas to believe in.

"Yes, Greg is a wonderful man," the Hare Krishna – who had been listening, as mesmerized as the players – added. "He is my friend. Of course, now his name is" – I forget what it was, but there were tons of rhythmic syllables.

Then the Hare Krishna asked Jerry about our soccer team.

It was, as they say in education, a "teachable moment," and both the Hare Krishna and I seized it. Suddenly our players saw the Krishnas not as an alien sect, but as human beings. They felt a genuine connection to them. And – I could almost see their brains making these leaps – they thought, *If this could happen to Greg, what does it say about me? Could I become a Hare Krishna too?*

For the rest of the trip the players did not stop talking about the Hare Krishnas. (They also did not stop singing the Krishna theme song, that monotonal chant only George Harrison could love.) They saw me in a new light – *Hey, Dan coached a Hare Krishna guy!* – but realized that wasn't such a weird thing after all.

Talk about your good karma.

P.S. I told my new Hare Krishna friend to say hello to Greg for me. I always wondered if he did. Then, a decade later, Greg e-mailed me out of the blue. He had been driving through Westport, he wrote, when suddenly his thoughts turned to soccer and all the good times he had way back when. We got together a week later in New York City, where Greg filled me in on his life. After leaving the Hare Krishnas he had taught public school, but recently quit. He was about to open a nouvelle cuisine restaurant. Dressed from head to toe in trendy black – shirt and pants, no robe -- he looked quite the part.

And yes, he said, the Hare Krishna my team met had indeed told him I said hello. It was one of the things he remembered most fondly from those long-ago days in Harvard Square.

TRAVEL TALES

There may be eight million stories in the Naked City, but after hauling soccer teams around the world I've got eight billion. (Fewer than half involve nakedness.) Here are several.

My very first trip was, I realize now, a learning experience for me at least as much as the players. I was in my mid-20s, but I'd already taken teams as far as Florida and Toronto (and lived to tell the tale). Europe would pose an infinitely greater challenge.

The first problem had nothing to do with soccer. Several key athletes were also Babe Ruth baseball stars. Their managers, facing the prospect of having to find other boys to stand around in the hot sun doing nothing for many innings over a two-week period, threatened that any boy who went to Europe with us would be disqualified from all baseball for the rest of the summer. I was vilified by the baseball establishment for having the audacity to plan a trip outside the "real" soccer season (fall, which is when the high school teams played). Soccer parents expected me to wave a magic bat and come up with a solution to allow their children to do everything. I think they wanted me to charter transatlantic flights to ferry the boys back and forth to their baseball commitments.

As always, the players themselves knew best. The managers' Ty Cobb-like obstinacy backfired when the kids said, well, it doesn't take a brainiac to choose between fielding grounders in Westport or cruising around Europe with my soccer buddies. The Neanderthal baseball managers lost; the soccer players won (as did the baseball benchwarmers, who became starters when our players quit Babe Ruth en masse).

The next problem came when our 10 p.m. departure was delayed nearly five hours by an oxygen leak. The boys decided that the 300 or so other passengers needed an alternative to sleeping on hard airport seats, so they entertained them by juggling soccer balls and tossing Frisbees. Today I would put a quick end to such frivolity, but hey, I was just a kid myself. I thought it was amusing. I also thought the passengers deserved what they got, because they were not exhibiting a ton of common sense. At one point two players commandeered the ticket counter (the gate agents had fled hours before). And even though they looked exactly like what they were – 15-year-old boys – an inordinate number of passengers came up asking travel-related questions.

"Do you know long the delay will be?" one woman wondered.

"Well, ma'am, as we explained earlier, it's an oxygen leak problem. These things can take a while to fix, and we want to make sure everything is perfect before we make another announcement," my starting right midfielder proclaimed.

"What about my connection in Paris?" a man asked.

"We're working as hard as we can to coordinate with all the airlines," responded my central defender. I was sure the next person would ask for a cockpit tour, and my kids would give it.

The entire scene might have been even funnier had I not realized I would spend the next eight hours in a confined space with adults who thought teenage soccer players were legitimate airline representatives.

Finally we boarded. My midfielder and defender assured me the oxygen leak was taken care of, and at 2:30 a.m. we took off. I urged the boys to fall asleep; I might as well have told them to solve Fermat's Last Theorem. Our wheels were barely up when the flight attendants rolled by with Cokes. At 3 a.m. they served dinner; breakfast followed three hours later. Thank god airplanes have ceilings; otherwise our players would have shot into the sky.

The three-hour layover in Paris drained them, however, and they finally conked out on the 50-minute hop to Zurich. They revived only slightly during the 40-minute drive to Konstanz, where our hosts – in a rare display of German inefficiency – had waited several hours for a welcoming ceremony.

We were greeted effusively. We received itineraries, city maps, bus tickets and other goodies, then were packed off with our host families for a good rest. However, most of our kids were so keyed up that they spent the night chatting with their new friends. We gathered for training at 10 the next morning: a sluggish, unenthusiastic bunch. I berated them for their lack of effort, whereupon one boy snarled, "Hey, Dan, it's like 4 a.m. back in Westport." He had a point.

That afternoon we were officially welcomed to Konstanz. (Germans are big on welcoming ceremonies. We must have been welcomed a dozen times on that trip in every burg we visited, including the day we left. "I think they're trying to prove they're not going to kill us," one of our players said, thankfully out of our greeter's earshot.)

It took our group a while to grow accustomed to European manners. The boys left Coke cans everywhere, talked louder than the residents of nursing homes, and thought nothing of slouching against parked cars. (Of all the Americans' rudenesses, that lounging upset the Germans the most. It was also the hardest habit to break.)

The boys did feel guilty about their thoughtless transgressions, because our Konstanz hosts had raised hospitality to almost comic levels. For example, one of the adults accompanying our team along brought his wife and two daughters. The family that hosted them moved their own two sons out of the house, just to accommodate their guests. After a week the American couple decided to give the German couple a break from the constant chauffeuring, tour-guiding and feeding, and took off for a day themselves. When they returned Herr Reisman took the American father aside, offered a drink and asked in a worried tone, "What have we done wrong? How have we offended you? Why did you not want to be with us today?"

At times, their concern for us veered toward the bizarre. On a hike in the Alps, a German woman accompanying us fell and broke her wrist. The bone pushed through the skin and she was clearly in pain, but that did not deter our hosts from stopping at a small cabin to grill wursts and feed us Cokes. We protested, but in vain. "The boys come first!" the German men declared. "She can go to the hospital when we get to the bottom. All is okay!"

"Ja, ja," she nodded, painfully.

Many of the German men took vacation time to be with the boys, and we learned that a number of parents had spent months studying English so they could communicate with us. (Our German, by contrast, consisted of *danke, bitte,* and *gesundheit.*) Our hosts paid for all our outings, and every meal. On top of that they showered us with gifts: books, pennants, shirts, jackets, pens. They asked nothing in return.

Everything was done quietly, graciously, sincerely. But every so often, despite our ear-to-ear grins, they would ask: "Is everything all right? Are you having a good time?" We would gush our replies: Oh yes, the land is so beautiful; the people are so friendly; the activities are great. And they would reply, "That is good. We do not know. We live here all the time, so you must tell us."

So it went, 15 days of climbing mountains; touring castles, churches and villages; traveling around Lake Constance and up the Rhine by ship, ferry, bus and car. Our boys did exceptionally well. They ran up a 7-1-1 record, including a victory in a tournament (organized for our benefit, of course), and earned unexpected praise from the Europeans. They complimented our skills (grudgingly), our strength and stamina (robustly). "You boys climb mountains all day, go out at night, play 80 minutes of soccer and still be ready to play 80 more," said one German father.

But the real stories of that trip were the amazing things that happened off the field. One of the most incredible events occurred in

Winterthur, Switzerland, following a soccer match we won handily. We piled into cars for the short trip back to Konstanz, but drove only a short distance before pulling up at a nice restaurant. Inside were the Swiss players. They had planned a sit-down dinner for us – and paid for it entirely themselves. It was a wonderful, unexpected event; we were overwhelmed. And then, as we said our *auf wiedersehen*s, the Winterthur boys presented each of our players with a Swiss Army knife.

Frantically, I dug around for a few T-shirts to reciprocate. Clearly we were amateurs at this hospitality game. That night, I learned one of the most important lessons of my coaching career: When traveling overseas, you can never have enough gifts.

From my next trip on, I never left home without a trunk full of goodies to give away.

Yet somehow I always returned to America with more than I handed out.

My dozen-plus overseas trips – only a few of which I have described so far -- taught me many other lessons. For example:

There is no better way to experience the world than through the eyes of teenagers.

They observe so much – differences in transportation, music, architecture, habits – even if they cannot always articulate what they see. Sometimes they can, however, and then it is a joy to hear. After noting that European drivers are much more polite than Americans, one boy asked, "Is it because their cars are smaller, they're more into walking than us, they're not in such a hurry, or they don't have to prove they're 'the man' to everyone?" Being privy to such thoughts makes me feel as if I am waiting for an oyster to open up. It does not happen often, but when it does a pearl appears.

The first rule of travel – expect the unexpected, then embrace it – is as true for teenagers as everyone else. For many boys the most unexpected aspect of a trip -- the home stay -- is also the most anxiety-provoking. No matter how many times I assure the players that they will be treated well – pampered, even – they have no idea what lies ahead. Once, at the end of a noisy 12-hour ride heading toward a home stay, our bus grew uncharacteristically silent. A boy turned to me and let his adolescent defenses down. "I'm really, really nervous," he admitted.

Within minutes of arriving, however, all fears evaporated. For three days our Danish hosts opened their homes and hearts to us. No request was too trivial, no article of clothing too clean to wash, no meal less than exquisitely prepared. Thousands of miles from home, suburban American boys learned the true meaning of community. It was as if they stepped into a 19th century Great Plains town where everyone knew everyone else, looked out for each other, and had time to talk and eat and work and laugh together. For the rest of their lives, the players on that trip – and those who participated in similar home stays – will not fear strangers.

You never know what will come next – or out of the mouths of kids. One morning, flying to Miami for the Junior Orange Bowl Tournament, I headed to the lavatory. When I returned, I saw that the flight attendants had passed out champagne – this was a special Delta Champagne Brunch promotion, so you can tell how long ago *that* was – and all of the 14-year-old boys sat expectantly, with full champagne glasses. One of the more glib players had convinced the flight attendants, who must have still been in the "I'm Debbie, Fly Me!" generation, that I wouldn't mind.

"Is it okay, Dan?" the leader of the pack asked expectantly.

"Yes," I said, to their amazement. Then I zinged them: "But there's one condition. If you want champagne, you have to drink all of it."

"All *riiiight!*" he said. He stood in the aisle, and offered a toast. "To Woog! To us! To the Orange Bowl Tournament!"

The boys clinked glasses, as they'd seen their parents do. They started to drink. And, as I knew they would, they gagged.

"Whoa!" "This is nasty!" "This stuff sucks!" And, of course, the inevitable question arose: "Dan, do we have to drink this?"

"Of course not," I said. "But here's a little lesson for you all: Be careful what you wish for. It might come true."

The flight attendants cleared off 15 full champagne glasses. They were not too pleased, but I figured they needed to learn a lesson too, this one about not succumbing to the pleas of 14-year-old boys. Apparently they understood, because on their next pass through they offered sodas.

"Can I have coffee?" the smallest boy asked.

The flight attendant seemed surprised. With the champagne fiasco fresh in her mind, she said, "Are you going to drink it?

He looked her square in the eye. "No," he said. "I'm going to open up this window, and dump it 30,000 feet in the air."

Freedom, Kris Kristofferson once wrote, is just another word for nothing left to lose. I see it differently. From the day we begin planning a trip, I tell the players that my assistant coach and I will give them as much freedom as they prove they can handle – and even less than they can imagine if they show they cannot. The result: They learn with stunning rapidity how to read a Swedish trolley map, how to budget foreign currency so as not to go broke the third day, and how to enjoy their independence without taking (too much) advantage of it.

The more freedom they get, the more the boys respect it. They laugh each time they see another American team – and at tournaments there are dozens of them – being led around by drill sergeant fathers, pulled back by hovering mothers. They feel sorry for teams that play only soccer, and never explore cities and cultures on their own. "They might as well go to Hershey Park," one boy scoffed. Too often in the United States, teenagers have no chance to show they can exist, even flourish, on their own. Given the opportunity, they prove they will always come through.

My players' adventurous spirit does not, sadly, extend to food. I grew profoundly more disappointed at the number of meals being eaten at McDonald's (and equally chagrined at the number of McDonald's to choose from, but that's another book). The boys rationalized their gustatory timidity by saying the ubiquitous fast food restaurants were the cheapest places to eat, but I believe they would have gone there even if they had to pay a king's ransom in euros. Finally I banned fast food restaurants – an unenforceable edict, to be sure, but one that eased the number of burgers consumed. I believe there was a salutary side effect in fitness and skills as well. Of course, whenever I mentioned it, the players rolled their eyes as if I were a very old nutritionist stuck in the 1950s.

Two European treats that always hit the spot, though, are Nutella and gelato. One boy once rationed himself to "only" three gelatos a day, and proclaimed himself so happy that if he got killed by a Vespa (not inconceivable, considering the carelessness of both Italian drivers and American street-crossers), he would die happy.

One more food story, this one about the time I had the good and bad fortune to be hosted by a German family that loved to eat (which hardly narrows it down). *Frau* was always cooking, *Herr* was always consuming what she'd cooked, and both her and herr were always concerned that I hadn't had enough. The meals were great, if heavy, but the portions would have choked a sumo wrestler. And at 5-2, 110 pounds, I have never been confused with a sumo wrestler. I suppose I should have learned the German expression for "No thank you, if I ate another crumb my insides would explode all over your nice apartment." Instead I just rubbed my stomach while pretending to smile.

The final morning I awoke to the smells of a bountiful breakfast. Eggs, cereal, fresh bread, fresh meat, fresh cheese – whatever anyone in Germany had ever eaten for breakfast was piled on my plate. I did a quick calculation – *be polite, eat as much as possible, give copious thanks, then skip the next four regularly scheduled meals* – and dug in. I plowed through a bit of everything. It took two solid hours. At last I patted my stomach, stifled a huge belch, said my *"danke"*s and got ready to finish packing.

My hosts looked hurt. "Why are you leaving the table?" *Frau* asked. "You must have lunch before you go!" And promptly rolled out another full meal, twice as large as the first.

Contrary to myth, the teenagers I travel with do appreciate history. They may not know every detail of the House of Orange, or why, when and how the intricate Scandinavian rivalries developed, but who in America does? What the boys do understand is that the magnificent castles we visit predate any U.S. edifice by centuries, even millennia; that European city streets are narrow, winding and cobblestoned for reasons having nothing to do with cuteness, and everything to do with time and place; and that -- despite what pop culture and modern media would have them believe – the United States is not the center of the universe.

Nothing beats watching the World Cup overseas. I was fortunate to do this three separate times, and each experience was remarkable. In 1982 we sat in a soccer clubhouse in West Germany when that nation and France tangled in one of the most memorable World Cup matches ever. Three televisions were all tuned to different stations – German, Swiss and Austrian – and although we could not understand the commentary on any of them, we were swept up in the passion of the long match. For 90 pulsating minutes, a 30-minute overtime featuring four goals, and the first-ever penalty kick shootout, our boys thrilled to the undeniable power soccer holds over the entire planet. After the players returned to the States and attempted to explain the World Cup to parents and friends who had no idea what the boys had been part of, some were reduced to tears.

In 1990 we were in Italy two weeks after the Cup ended. Like sweet perfume, however, excitement lingered in the air. More tangibly, the streets of Verona were lined with enormous flags bearing the World Cup logo. My first thought was that our players were fully capable of trying to "liberate" them as souvenirs; then I realized the banners were so huge, and tied so securely to the tops of high light poles, that even such an intrepid group as mine would not try. So I did not warn them against it; why put ideas in their head, I reasoned. On the plane home, as they shared what-really-went-on secrets with me, I learned that the final night they indeed made a valiant attempt to do just what I feared. (The local *polizia* put a quick end to the stunt, when the boys were a mere 20 feet into their climb.) They added that the plan was to present the flag to me as a gift. I told them I was touched – I guess – but I should not have spoken so quickly. "Yeah," the leader of the gang said. "We figured you were the only one who had room in his luggage to get it home."

In 1998 we were in Europe during two key matches. For weeks back in Connecticut, our players had seen the tournament unwind. They watched every afternoon match, then raced to training to dissect what they had seen. These boys were as caught up in World Cup fever as any group I'd seen.

Naturally, they were delighted to find themselves in the historic Dutch city of Maastricht the night Holland and Brazil squared off in the semifinal. Everyone crowded into a bar; even the most rabid Brazil fans among us turned Orange. We shared the ups and downs with throngs of Dutchmen through 120 minutes of 1-1 action, then agonized as two penalty kick saves thwarted Holland's attempt to reach the finals for the first time in 20 years. When the game ended, the silent streets described the pain of an entire nation more than any words ever could.

Five days later we were in Gothenburg, Sweden. We had arrived by ferry just a few hours earlier, but watching the final was more important than getting ready for our first Gothia Cup match the next morning. We joined 12,000 other soccer fans in an enormous indoor ice rink, where the match was televised on giant screens. The commentary was in Swedish, so we had no idea why the great Ronaldo played so poorly – he suffered either an epileptic seizure or anxiety attack a few hours before the match, we learned later from the English press – but no translation was necessary to appreciate the brilliance of playmaker Zinedine Zidane, the fierceness of keeper Fabien Barthez, or the dominance of France as it cruised to a 3-0 shutout over favored Brazil. To me, the essence of the World Cup is sitting amid 12,000 screaming spectators from around the world in a Swedish ice rink, watching France play Brazil. *"Jogo bonito,"* *c'est magnifique!*

I always hope that, when in Gudumholm, my players will do as the Gudumholmans do. Of course, I try to model that behavior myself.

Our Danish hosts went so far out of their way for us, I thought they would end up on another continent. It's nearly impossible to reciprocate such astonishing hospitality, and though they certainly appreciated the plaques, pennants, flags, autographed soccer balls, photo books about New England and other gifts we give them, it never seemed to me to be enough.

So I decided to speak Danish.

I am not, of course, a fluent Danish speaker. Like most Americans who attended school in the 1960s and '70s, my foreign language skills consist of random words like *bonjour, ciao* and *Beck's.* However, I vowed to give something back to these wonderful people who had done so much for us.

I wrote a speech in Danish.

Okay, to be honest, I wrote it in English. But Torsten, the teenage boy in the family I was staying with, translated it into Danish. Then he spoke the words, and I transcribed them phonetically.

This was not easy. Danish has been described (by the Danes' ancient rivals, the Swedes, with a bit of inter-Scandinavian humor) as "not a language, but a speech impediment." I will not argue. There is no way to write down on paper the sound of someone about to huck a huge ball of mucus from the back of his throat, or pucker his tongue as if sucking on a dozen lemons. Those noises form the foundation of spoken Danish. But I gave it my best shot.

I practiced all afternoon. I spit, I gagged, I contorted my facial muscles into positions I never knew existed. It sounded like gibberish to me, but Torsten assured me he understood what I was attempting to say. He better have; he'd written the damn thing.

That night, the final dinner seemed like a potlatch – the old Puget Sound ritual where Native Americans feasted, danced, told stories and, most importantly, tried to give away more gifts than they got in return. Nearly everyone in the town of Gudumholm made a speech. We Americans understood everything, of course, because they were Danish and thus spoke English better then we did. Our captain thanked the hosts.

Suddenly it was my turn.

I stood, speech in hand, and began. I wish I could repeat here what I said there, but unfortunately the only copy of my text now sits in the Gudumholm Hall of Fame. Thankfully, my hucking, tongue-twisting and facial contorting did not go in vain. My players – who had no idea this was coming – listened more than they ever had before to me, though this time they could not understand a word. The Danish players and parents were – I admit it – mesmerized. Whether this was because my Danish reached their hearts and souls, or because they had never heard their language mangled so brutally, I have no idea. I did see tears on one or two faces – again, whether from genuine emotion or magnificently repressed laughter, I do not know. Suffice it to say, when I finished they applauded thunderously.

I sat down, relieved the ordeal was over and proud I had done my part for American-Danish relations.

Though looking back, the massive quantities of Tuborg we were all drinking probably had a lot to do with it too.

Fortunately, in all my trips abroad I have faced only two injuries serious enough to go to a hospital. Both left me shaking my head incredulously at health care, Europe-style.

The first occurred in Germany when a boy jammed his wrist. It might have been broken; it may only have been sprained. It was not a major emergency by any stretch of the imagination. But when I got to the local hospital and started speaking in English, it was as if I had accompanied a patient in the midst of a massive coronary.

Receptionists, nurses, orderlies, doctors, all scurried about to help. The waiting room was filled with more serious cases – I remember a bleeding man who appeared to have been in a horrible traffic accident – but the Germans insisted on moving my player to the head of the line. "You are our guests!" the head nurse said. "Please, let us help you!"

I thought everyone in the emergency room was a "guest," but there is no arguing with a German woman who has made up her mind. My player was X-rayed, had his wrist cast (it was indeed broken), given pain medication and sent on his way, all in 20 minutes. And when I offered the extensive medical and insurance forms I always carry with me, they stared at me as if I had 12 heads.

"Do not worry!" I was told. "We will send the bill to America. Bye-bye."

Several months later, the boy's parents did indeed receive the bill. It came to $9.50.

The second incident occurred in Denmark. A player sprained his ankle badly. Once again, hospital officials whipped us into the examining room. The ankle was assessed, wrapped and treated. Before we left, the doctor handed our player a pair of crutches.

I waved them off. "That's okay," I said. "We're leaving for Sweden tomorrow, and won't be able to return them."

Once again, I got the 12-headed look. "So keep them!" the doctor said. "After all, they are only crutches."

This time, the player never received a bill at all. Had he gotten those crutches at an emergency room in the States, his parents would have been out a couple hundred bucks. And if he mentioned he was leaving the next day, the doctor would have yanked the crutches back so fast the boy would have sprained his other ankle too.

Before we leave on any trip, I tell the parents that although we will be gone only two weeks, their son will return home much more than two weeks older. This is not always as figurative a concept as it seems. One mother called me a day or two after we got back. She said she had not understood what I meant about growing more than two weeks older until her son walked out of customs and into the terminal. She had not recognized him. "Yeah," I joked. "His hair got pretty long, and that beard looked pretty scruffy."

"No," she said seriously. "I don't mean it that way. I really didn't know it was him. I've never seen him carry himself with such confidence before. For the first time in his life, he looked like a man."

That was the second nicest compliment I've gotten after a trip. The best has been repeated many times, by many players, but I never tire of hearing it. On the plane home, and for weeks afterward, boys tell me, "I can't wait to travel on my own." They say they look forward to returning to Europe a year or two later, perhaps traveling to South America, Africa or Asia, with backpacks, guy friends or girlfriends, a few bucks and no plan beyond seeing much, much more of this fascinating planet. Whenever I hear that, I know that the number of games we won (or players we lost) is irrelevant. By the most important standard – personal growth -- the trip was a smash.

GARRETT

Here's something they don't teach in coaching school: There are kids you dislike.

I don't mean "find difficult to deal with." These are not youngsters who arrive habitually late, require more than their share of attention or have no acquaintance with personal hygiene. I'm talking about actual dislike. It's not pretty, nor is it particularly professional, but it's true. Unless you're Jesus Christ himself, during your career you will coach a few players you wouldn't mind seeing on someone else's squad. (And in this day and age even Coach Christ's players would complain about their positions, and parents would form email petitions to demand His removal for failure to use the "right" formation.)

I did not start out disliking Garrett. He was actually charming at first, in a goofy ninth grader sort of way. But the next year he turned 16, grew taller and stronger and bolder, became the leader of a group of popular kids, realized he knew more about everything than everyone else, failed to make varsity, developed a chip on his shoulder larger than the Starship Enterprise, and proceeded to make life miserable for his parents, teachers and me. Particularly me, since I saw him for more hours each day than any of his teachers, or for that matter his parents.

A typically dramatic moment in the Dan and Garrett Wars occurred midway through his second junior varsity season. We were playing a fun 3-v-1 warm-up game; if you were the one, defending a small cone, you did five pushups for every goal the three scored on you. We're not talking Simon Legree here. Games like this need a bit of motivation to keep players' interest and skill level high, and most players knock off 10 or 15 pushups, while their teammates give them a good-natured hard time.

Not Garrett. His half-hearted effort earned him a quick 30 pushups; then he grew frustrated, so instead of winning the ball to end his "round," he stopped playing. His opponents moved in for the kill. The more they scored, the lazier Garrett got. The lazier he got, the angrier I became. "Thirty-five!" "*Forty!*" "*FORTY-FIVE!*" "**FIFTY!**" Garrett quickly worked himself into Parris Island territory.

Somewhere near 100, he simply stopped playing. I was incensed. "Ninety-five pushups!" I yelled. *"Do 'em now!"*

"*NO!*" Garrett screamed back, fusing his own rage with mine.

I don't know what English word means "more incensed than ever," but I was it. I was mad at myself for letting the situation get out of hand, and mad at the team for standing around watching – not playing – just waiting to see which of these two incredibly stubborn people would win the battle of wills. Most of all, though, I was mad at Garrett. What a fucking asshole.

"Garrett, you've got 95 pushups. You better do them now!" I shrieked.

"You can't make me!" he retorted. If that sounds like he was throwing a 2-year-old's temper tantrum, he was. I barely stopped myself from descending to his level and replying, "Can too!"

The reason I didn't was because he was already in full stride. Garrett was actually leaving practice, walking across the field with his back to me. He continued purposefully all the way up a hill, across another field, through a parking lot, and on into the woods. If it was a movie, the audience would have been riveted by the beauty and drama of the shot.

But this was more real than a movie; it was a junior varsity soccer practice. I spent a few seconds feeling sorry for myself – no one had ever walked out on my practice before – when suddenly my coaching brain kicked in. Uh oh – what if something happens to Garrett? If he threw a rock through the school window, got hit by a car on his way home, or took his father's shotgun – did I mention his dad was an avid hunter, and animal heads filled the house? – and blew his brains out, I'd be dead. I was in charge, legally if not at that precise moment emotionally. Besides, 20 witnesses would back their socially powerful friend rather than their tweaked-out coach ("Geez, I don't know, Dan seemed to lose it there for a while"). If I was 16, I would have turned on me too.

So I deputized Garrett's best friend. "Go get him!" I barked. "Tell him he better come back!"

"I'll try," the boy said without conviction, and trotted off. I think he was happy not to stick around for the next eruption of Mt. Vesuvius.

He returned half an hour later, minus Garrett of course. Practice continued, but playing soccer was difficult with everyone running on eggshells. It was a completely wasted day, and hardly my finest hour.

I called Garrett that night. He said all the right things about being stupid and hot-headed, though it was hard to tell how sorry he truly was because each apology was prefaced with and followed by a long dissertation on how unfair I was, how stupid the 3-v-1 game was, and basically what a douche bag I was. He didn't use that precise term, but the implication was clear.

Garrett and I spent the rest of the year in an uneasy truce – imagine John McCain serving in Barack Obama's cabinet, or Robert E. Lee taking orders from Ulysses Grant. I am always sorry to see a soccer season end, but in this case the joy of being rid of Garrett far outweighed the sorrow of packing up the balls and infamous cones.

Call me stupid, call me stubborn, call me a douche bag, but don't call me vindictive. That's why I never thought about leaving Garrett off the team that would go to Europe the following spring. He was a long-time member of that team, and (even if he could not defend 3-v-1 to save his life) a good player. Besides, all his friends were going. Finally, if I did not include him, his mother might come after me with one of her husband's shotguns. She was not the type to miss.

But the intervening months did not mellow Garrett. If anything, springtime made him even more obstreperous. Once again, training sessions and games overflowed with tension. He questioned why we were doing whatever we were doing, and who was playing where and when. I believed as the coach I did not have to justify every decision; he believed as a player he had a right to voice his opinions. I saw a player who was moping around, not working hard, and needed a good kick in the butt; he saw a 16-year-old who was still growing rapidly, felt a bit gawky, and was trying as hard as he could, even though the coach was always on his case. I brought out the worst in Garrett; he returned the favor for me.

School ended, June morphed into July, and the players looked more and more forward to departure. With each passing day, meanwhile, I grew more concerned. I could not imagine spending two weeks responsible for someone I loathed. One night, I actually had a nightmare about Garrett.

The Saturday before we left, when training was over, I spilled my concerns to my assistant, Jerry. (Yes, this is the same Jerry who, a decade earlier, had tormented the Hare Krishnas in Harvard Square, then was stupefied to learn I had actually coached one of them a while before. If you have not read that chapter yet, do so now.) One of the reasons I selected Jerry as my assistant was because of the Hare Krishna affair: He had the capacity to absorb life's lessons, and grow as human being. He also possessed several other important qualities: a willingness to overlook my idiosyncrasies, the ability to interpret my views to teenagers at those not infrequent times I did not explain myself particularly well, and most importantly a sense of humor.

I remember the exact words I used with him that day in the parking lot: "Jerry, I can't go with Garrett to Europe. I hate him. It's either him or me." I guess I did not want to mince words, or maybe I hoped Jerry would agree.

Instead, he laughed. "C'mon, Dan," he said. "You don't really hate him." Jerry was 24 years old, just two years out of college, and it probably never occurred to him that a coach could hate a player.

"I do. I hate his guts."

Jerry laughed again, a bit nervously this time. He was beginning to understand I was serious, though it was beyond his comprehension that I could consider either firing a player, or not going to Europe myself. He was seeing a side of his former coach that was not exactly pleasant; at the same time he recognized he might play a significant role in this drama. Jerry liked Garrett; he saw in him a kindred spirit, an intelligent goofball who loved the game but at the same time took neither it nor the coach too seriously.

"Let me talk to him," Jerry suggested.

"Fine," I said. "Say whatever you want. But you have to let him know he's got to clean up his act. I refuse to spend two weeks in Europe worrying about what he's going to say or do, when's the next time he's going to blow up, or how he's going to embarrass me or the team."

That too was fine with Jerry. Then I had a brainstorm. "In fact, you can be in charge of him the whole time. He's your project. I don't care how you do it, but you're responsible for him."

You would have thought I'd given Jerry the keys to the soccer kingdom. He nodded gratefully. "You got it, Dan," he said. "Garrett's mine." He was already scheming, I could tell.

I think Jerry and Garrett went out to lunch the next day. I never asked what happened, that's how much I wanted Jerry to get Garrett out of my rapidly thinning hair. But whatever they talked about, it worked. Through the next few training sessions Jerry hovered near his project, playing Annie Sullivan to Garrett's Helen Keller. Jerry intercepted my instructions, heading off incipient anger at a stupid drill by using Garrett-speak to explain my logic. He modulated Garrett's emotions, keeping him on an even keel from the start of practice to finish. It was almost like what the Hare Krishnas had done to turn my former soccer player into a religious fanatic, but it succeeded. Garrett smiled more, Jerry eased off and returned to working with the rest of the team, and the pounding headaches that had plagued me for weeks disappeared.

A few days later we were once again one big happy team. On the plane to Amsterdam I walked down the aisle, headed to the restroom. Garrett stretched back in his seat in a typical pose that, only because it was his, would a week earlier have driven me berserk. His way-too-loud headphones leaked indistinguishable but annoying sounds. His hands thumped on the arm rests, while his long legs kicked the seat in front.

I was about to ignore him – after all, it was now Jerry's job to teach him proper airplane etiquette -- when suddenly he reached out, touched my arm and turned down his "music." For the first time in a year, he smiled at me. "Thanks for taking me, Dan," he said with emotion. "We haven't even gotten there yet, but already this is the coolest thing I've done. I had a boner all week just thinking about it."

This was perhaps not the most elegant way of describing anticipation, especially on a crowded plane, but it was certainly honest. It was also typical Garrett. Suddenly, I realized my feelings were changing. How could you hate a kid who comes out with a line like that?

"Thanks," I said. "I'm glad you're here too."

Those were magic words. The animosity of the past year melted away. Garrett and I were, if not on the same page, at least reading similar books. Maybe the next two weeks would not be so gruesome after all.

The acid test came sooner than I expected. It was our first full day in Holland, and despite jet lag we trained intensely with one of the country's top coaches. The players rose to the challenge: The man's excellent English, simple yet elegant training methods, and boundless enthusiasm had the boys improving by the minute.

Near the end of the morning Garrett asked if he could go to the bathroom. Of course, I said magnanimously; I pointed to a locker area in a corner of the park. Garrett loped away; it was clear he did not want to miss any more of the session than he had to.

Three minutes later he reappeared. But something was wrong: His face was ashen, and fear filled his eyes. Garrett's hands were actually shaking.

"It wasn't my fault!" he stuttered. "I swear it wasn't! It just happened! Dan, I swear it just happened!"

I could not believe what I was hearing. We had been there just 12 hours, and already there was trouble – from Garrett, of all people. Would our newfound amity come crashing down? And then I wondered: What actually happened? How exactly could he have screwed up in three minutes?!

"It's a flood!" was all Garrett could blurt. "Come here quick!"

I would like to say my mind made clever, we're-in-Holland-so-there-must-be-a-little-boy-with-his-hand-in-the-dike associations, but it did not. All I thought about was what kind of a flood there could be, whether Garrett had caused it, and how I had to keep cool no matter what. *There are two sides to every story, two sides to every story, two sides to every story...*if I repeated that mantra enough times, I might start believing it.

Garrett had not exaggerated. The flood in the locker room was of biblical proportions. Water cascaded out of a broken pipe over the sink; it was already several inches high, and rising rapidly.

"All I did was turn on the faucet!" Garrett said. "I swear to God, that's all I did!"

It was clear he had not vandalized the place; it was also clear the North Sea was spewing into the bathroom. I like to think I can solve most soccer-related problems, but here I was clearly – and almost literally – over my head.

We raced back to the Dutch coach. He gave the players a water break (!), then jogged over to assess the damage. He heard the flood before he saw it; when he peered inside, his reaction was both welcome and typically Dutch. He threw back his head and laughed.

"Ah, a flood!" he said. "Yes, this is a problem." Then he laughed again.

He picked up his cell phone, and spoke rapidly. Dutch is not the most beautiful language (unless compared with German), but it was clear from his tone he was not angry. Several times he made wave motions with his hands, even though his caller could not see. Apparently the situation was more amusing than dire.

Garrett stood by, his mouth agape. Neither the Dutch coach nor the American was angry. Garrett had not created an international incident; he had not even screwed up. No one was mad at him. This would be a great trip, after all.

And it was. Jerry kept a close eye on Garrett, though he no longer had to; now they were friends, not zookeeper and wild elephant. Garrett made sure to hang out with me too. He went out of his way to offer food, sit next to me on trolleys, even ask if I was having fun. I reciprocated. It was clear Garrett was having the time of his life. Best of all, he gave me no more updates on his state of arousal.

What is especially gratifying is that today, years later, Garrett – now a successful young businessman, and of all things an MBA – works hard to keep in touch. Every so often he calls, e-mails, even appears at my door. Sometimes he just says hi; at other times he asks for advice. The issues – career moves, finding a relationship in a big city, reaching a balance between personal and professional happiness – are a bit more important than fixing a broken pipe. But even if Garrett just wanted to know if I'd seen any good movies lately, I'd feel honored he asked. He certainly has grown up.

Then again, so have I.

THE BEST SEAT IN GIANTS STADIUM

The rain fell in buckets, through the entire match. Playing soccer in a downpour is never easy; doing it on old-fashioned artificial turf was nearly impossible. But the team of 12-year-olds adapted nicely to the conditions. Being cheered on by a crowd of over 73,000 didn't hurt.

It sounds like a pre-teen's fantasy, but it was one of the most real, most memorable moments of my adult life. More than a quarter century after it happened, I remember it as if it were yesterday.

My team was playing the preliminary match, before the New York Cosmos met the Rochester Lancers in the North American Soccer League championship semifinals. The site was Giants Stadium, the gleaming New Jersey edifice that had opened just a few months before. Throughout the spring and summer, crowds grew almost exponentially. It was the last of Pele's three seasons with the Cosmos. The team, with a mind-boggling cast including Franz Beckenbauer, Carlos Alberto, Giorgio Chinaglia and a host of other international stars, had captured New York's fancy. Mick Jagger and fellow glitterati hung out in private boxes; artist Leroy Neiman and a lady friend picnicked on the field (complete with white linen and red wine), and all of the Meadowlands was hotter than New York's trendy new nightclub, Studio 54.

My press pass enabled me to join in the excitement. Through the Westport soccer mafia -- Cosmos communications director Mark Brickley was a friend and former high school teammate – two of the squads I coached caught the fever too. Mark slotted us in for several preliminary matches. All year long we watched the crowds swell. I thought nothing could top the July afternoon when the temperature on the artificial surface was so intense, the soles of the boys' soccer shoes became unglued.

Yet even that could not have prepared me for that steamy, rainy August night. The details of our preliminary match are lost in the mists of time; besides, nothing could be more irrelevant than whether a U-12 team won or lost a warm-up game. However, what happened after our appearance will remain etched in my mind forever.

We headed toward the steps that would take us into the stands, back to anonymity. At the other end of the stadium the Cosmos and Lancers waited to emerge from the tunnel, and 73,000-plus eyes were focused there. But as the guards opened the security gate for us to pass through, I stopped. "Look around, guys," I told the team. "This is a sight you will never forget."

It was heart-stopping. Rain cascaded down; with the stadium lights on we could not only feel how hard it was pouring, we could *see* it. The lights illuminated the nearly full house. We stood on the grass – artificial, but what the hell – of what at that moment was the newest, most modern stadium in the United States. And the reason all those people were there, clapping, screaming and stamping their feet, oblivious to the downpour, was *soccer.* It was a singular moment in American sports history, and I did not want my players to ever forget it.

Of course, I wanted to preserve the moment for myself, too.

Little did I know that less than two months later, those same boys and I would find ourselves in the same stadium, on the same soccer field. And who could have believed that at that next appearance we would be active participants in one of the greatest tributes in sports history.

October 1, 1977 was Pele's farewell game. The Cosmos had won the North American Soccer League championship, and now he was retiring for good. (His first retirement lasted one year, until Warner Communications, the Cosmos' deep-pocketed and forward-thinking owners, lured him from Brazil to help lead their team to the promised land.) A gala send-off was planned. Once again, my team got the call asking if we wanted to be part of the festivities.

Did we want to take part?! Perhaps the only stupider question to ask a 12-year-old soccer player is, "Would you rather play a game or have your head smashed repeatedly with a tire iron?"

We arrived hours ahead of schedule, both to beat the traffic and because we had to "practice." Nine youth teams were involved in the pre-game show. Players were to demonstrate ball skills; each of the nine captains would then hand Pele a bouquet of roses, before his speech. For two hours we underwent choreographic instruction on the practice turf a few hundred yards from the stadium. The field was shielded from view by green netting – not for our privacy, but for the principal users, the New York football Giants – so we were oblivious to the excitement building all around us.

At noon we were whisked through the parking lot and into the tunnels beneath the stadium. I had been there many times, in journalistic capacities, and it was always lively – only the Cosmos could draw celebrities to their locker room – but I had never seen it like this. Secret Service agents swarmed everywhere; President Carter's son Chip was arriving soon. Golf carts whizzed past, carrying celebrities like Frank Gifford and Jim McKay (the announcers for the game on ABC-TV). My players did not really care about Frank Gifford or Jim McKay – and even less about Chip Carter – but when Muhammad Ali appeared, they snapped to attention.

Just two days before he had won a 15-round decision over Earnie Shavers in New York, to retain the world heavyweight title. Dark glasses covered his banged-up eyes, yet he was unmistakably Muhammad Ali. He rose slowly from the golf cart, unfolded his massive body, and – in the way many people who spend years in public have perfected – began walking through the crowd, staring ahead without seeing anyone. It was clear he wanted to be left alone.

But that did not stop Pierre, a small African-American youngster on our team. "Hey! Ali!" he yelled.

The champ stopped, a few yards from Pierre. He glanced around to see who had called his name. His hands hung limply at his sides. And then – in a fraction of a split second, *muchquickerthanthis*, so instantaneously I literally could not see it – Muhammad Ali's right hand was on top of Pierre's head, caressing his 12-year-old Afro. With that faster-than-the-speed-of-light action, I realized the difference between heavyweight champions and everyone else who lives on this planet.

"Hey, brother," Ali acknowledged. Then, just as suddenly, he moved on.

He was gone before Pierre could register what happened. His teammates could not believe what happened either. They gaped at the spot where Muhammad Ali had just stood, then crowded around Pierre.

"I'm never going to wash my head again," he announced solemnly.

And that was just a preview of what lay ahead.

We were ushered onto the field. All 77,000 seats were filled. The anticipatory buzz created an odd rumble. At the center stripe dignitaries from all walks of life – sports, politics, entertainment – crowded onto a makeshift stage. TV cameras were everywhere; the event was broadcast around the world.

The nine youth teams that would demonstrate soccer skills took their places around the perimeter. We had been assigned the best spot of all: midfield, directly in front of the stage, closest to the action. (*Thanks again, Mark!*) Behind us, state troopers held back a throng of 700 photographers.

The nine teams were introduced. Seventy-seven thousand spectators watched the youngsters juggle, pass, dribble and shoot. Every boy was convinced 154,000 eyes – not to mention an international television audience of tens of millions – was on him alone. (In truth, we probably represented a good time for commercials, or at least a taped review of Pele's life.) Our boys performed admirably, even if their parents and I were the only ones who cared. The players came back to their assigned spots, smack by the stage, directly in front of the 700 photographers.

The speeches began. As the moment drew near for the captains to walk forward and present Pele with roses, I turned to our captain. Thomas was a nice, earnest kid who was probably seen as the team leader because he was the goalkeeper (and thus allowed to yell at his teammates), and because at 5-6 he towered over them. He took his captaincy seriously, and now he was about to do something billions of soccer fans across the globe could only dream about: He was going to give Pele some flowers.

I motioned Thomas over. "Listen," I said. "Look where we are. You're the closest of all the nine captains, so you'll get there first. Whatever you do, don't just shove the flowers at him and walk away. Hand him the flowers with your left hand, put out your right hand to shake his, then stay there for a few seconds. You never know what might happen."

Thomas nodded, but a petrified look crossed his face. "Wait!" he said. "What hand? What do I do? What should I say?"

I changed tactics. "Don't worry," I said. "Just give him the flowers, but stand there. And smile!"

Thomas picked up the flowers. His moment had come. He walked confidently to the stage. He arrived long before the others, as I knew he would. He handed the roses to Pele. Pele took them, stuck out his hand, and shook Thomas'. The other captains were still walking over. Pele put his hand on the back of Thomas's neck, and pulled him close. He leaned over – not too far, because he is not a big man, and Thomas was a big kid – and whispered in Thomas's ear. Behind me, 700 photographers went berserk. I had no idea how loud 700 auto-drives could be until they all went off simultaneously. The clickety-clack was deafening.

The other captains finally arrived at the stage. Pele released Thomas, and turned to accept eight more bouquets. Thomas walked quickly back to our team. The grin across his face seemed to stretch from one goalmouth to the other. Once again, the 700 photographers went into a shooting frenzy.

His teammates mobbed him. "That's so cool!" "Awesome!" "Holy shit!" they shouted.

I had a more adult reaction. "What did Pele say to you?" I asked.

Thomas looked at me, dumbfounded. He glanced back at the stage. Stricken, he turned to me once again. "I forget!" he said in a strangled voice.

The rest of the day was anticlimactic. Pele gave his now-famous farewell speech, ending with: "Say with me now three times: Love! Love! Love!" (Though with his Brazilian accent, and the vagaries of the stadium sound system, it sounded as if he was asking the crowd to shout three times "Ruv!") The celebrities trotted off, the stage was dismantled, and the game began. Pele played the first half with the Cosmos, the second with Santos (the club with which he spent most of his career). Fittingly, he scored – the 1281st goal of his career. At the end of the match, with the sun setting and the air growing chilly, the two teams carried him off the field on their shoulders, together.

I returned to Giants Stadium many times since October 1, 1977 – before it was demolished, for a newer, even better arena. For several years the Cosmos continued to fill the place; a later tenant, the crassly commercially named New York Red Bulls of Major League Soccer, came nowhere close. But in 1994 the World Cup was standing room only, and occasional exhibition matches generated 70,000-plus crowds too.

Nothing, however, remotely neared replicating that magical year of 1977. It was a time when professional soccer's future seemed limitless. Who knew that – nearly as quickly as it took for Thomas to forget what Pele had whispered in his ear – the dream of 77,000-filled American stadiums would vanish as well?

WILLKOMMEN IN KONSTANZ

Konstanz is truly beautiful. An ancient town on the coast of Germany's Lake Constance, once known for farming and vineyards but now a celebrated vacation spot, it was the very first place I visited in Europe. The Westport-Konstanz connection predated my own coaching career; my high school soccer coach and mentor, Albie Loeffler, had already established an exchange program with the Wollmatingen Football Club, and I merely continued the tradition of *freundschaft.*

It was hard not to love Konstanz. The ancient castles, wooden bridges and narrow streets gave it a European look right out of a story book. And Wollmatingen was a typical European soccer club too, with a lovingly maintained field, teams for all ages, and a well-worn clubhouse where everyone congregated to eat, drink, talk, drink, laugh, drink, watch matches and sing. Occasionally, they drank.

The people of Konstanz were overwhelmingly friendly. They opened their homes and hearts to us, their American "sport friends." I organized two trips to Konstanz; both times our team stayed for two weeks. Wollmatingen parents eagerly took vacation time, so they could devote themselves completely to us. Each morning when our players gathered together, they shared host family stories that sounded almost comical.

"My 'mother' sewed up all the holes in my socks," one boy would say.

"Yeah, well mine polishes my cleats every night," a second countered.

"That's nothing," a third piped up. "Mine blow-dries my hair for me in the morning!"

And so it went, day after day after day, as the good men and women of Konstanz toiled mightily to prove that "wurst" meant food, not a definition of national behavior.

But even though Konstanz is only a few steps – literally -- from the Swiss border, we were still on German soil. And sometimes, all the beer and *gemutlichkeit* couldn't hide the fact that this was a country that – not as long ago as we'd like to think – killed millions of people simply because they were Jewish.

Which made for a very interesting situation when Abe and Susan Silverman's host family invited them to an evening with Grandpa and Grandma.

Abe and Susan were parents of two boys who played for me. This time they were chaperones for their older child's team, although that description seems too formal. Abe was a psychologist, Susan a stay-at-home mother with organizational skills not seen since Eisenhower planned D-Day. Parentally they complemented each other perfectly, which is why – despite the fact that Abe was a shrink – their kids were happy, wholesome and not the least bit screwed up. Traveling with the Silvermans was actually fun, something I could not say about some soccer parents (see the chapter called "Mommies and Daddies" for that diatribe).

Abe and Susan practiced a fairly laissez-faire form of Judaism, which is why they were not freaked out at the prospect of spending two weeks in a German home. And though they were not big drinkers or partiers, they were adventurous and high-spirited enough to believe that, when in Konstanz, you did as the Konstanzdammers do. The Silvermans plunged into the life of the town, and every day Abe mined a different psychological nugget that explained why the Germans behaved as they did.

Toward the end of our stay, though, the Silvermans met their match. Their hosts, a generous and hospitable couple around the same age and socioeconomic status, stopped serving schnitzel and pouring drinks long enough to take their American friends to their own parents' home for schnitzel and drinks.

The evening went as swimmingly as could be expected, considering that the older couple did not speak English, and over the previous week and a half the Silvermans and their hosts had already plowed every conversational field they could imagine. But they persevered, and after schnapps Abe and Susan accepted their hosts' invitation for a tour of the house.

The Silvermans expressed proper admiration for the kitchen, bedroom and bathroom, then followed the grandparents downstairs. And there, amidst the bicycles, power tools and old sofas that fill basements everywhere in the world, stood a life-size mannequin. It occupied the center of the floor. A ceiling fixture bathed it in reverential light -- the better to see, from head to toe, the mannequin's full Nazi regalia. As Grandpa pointed out proudly, it was his very own military uniform.

Showing incredible restraint, the Silvermans neither shrieked nor fled. They managed to mumble something vague and unclear, walked upstairs, and seized the first opportunity to leave. On the way home they chatted with their host family about schnitzel and beer, saving their thoughts about the horror they had just witnessed for themselves. As a good therapist – and perhaps to ease their own intense discomfort – Abe tried to analyze the reasons why the grandfather had not only saved his uniform all these years, not only spotlighted it like a museum piece, but felt that a pair of 40-something Americans would actually enjoy seeing it. Abe made his living figuring out what goes through people's heads, but this case stumped him.

And try as he might, Abe could not put one thought out of his own head: "The man wearing that uniform could have killed some of my relatives."

For the rest of the trip, the food and drink seemed a little less tasty, the conversation a bit more forced, the jovial hospitality – well, just call it somewhat more Germanic.

Of course, adults are not the only ones who drink in Konstanz – or anywhere in Europe. For teenagers, "no drinking age" is as much a lure as high-quality soccer, cool castles and topless beaches. The lack of a drinking age is a myth, of course. Most European countries do have laws limiting alcohol consumption, though they are less restrictive and more loosely enforced than in the U.S. (the opposite of drivers' licenses, which in this country are handed out as easily as youth soccer trophies, while overseas they are as precious as plutonium).

But American teenagers don't want to hear about age restrictions. The lure of being 15 years old, able to walk into a bar and order a drink – just as all their lives they have seen older people do on TV and in movies – packs incalculable power. Something about Europe and alcohol sucks in the straightest, squarest, least likely teenagers. Trust me on this: You can't trust even your most devout Mormon, the one who's both an Eagle Scout and president of his Students Against Drunk Driving chapter. One night, under the influence of teammates, his host family and the free-wheeling lifestyle of Europe, he'll show up staggering under the influence of beer or wine. (In Spain, sangria.)

All you can hope is that he won't be as hammered as the five players I encountered one night on the streets of downtown Konstanz.

It was near the end of our trip, and we adults thought we had done a good job of keeping our players sober. If Konstanz's nickname is not "The Beer Garden City," it should be, and on several occasions our hosts had taken our team to one of their favorite spots for pre-game meals or post-game celebrations. (They would have taken us at halftime too, had there been a beer garden within jogging distance of the field.) Each time the waitresses came around, our players – none yet old enough to drive, even in the U.S. – made drinking motions with their thumbs and pinkies, and looked at us with hangdog expressions. No, we shook our heads. The boys rolled their eyes skyward, ordered Cokes which arrived in tiny cups, then watched enviously as their German counterparts drank beers from steins the size of U-boats.

Thus the other adults and I were not overly surprised when, around 10 p.m. one evening, our leisurely stroll was interrupted by the sight of several players enjoying their own night on the town. "Interrupted" is actually too mild a word; these boys were impossible to miss. Singing, dancing and playing imaginary instruments to oom-pah songs they were making up on the spot, they cut a less-than-direct path down the narrow sidewalk. They were accompanied by several teenagers from the Wollmatingen team, who probably had had much more to drink, but were far more able to hold their liquor. The Germans were delighted to see us. The American boys should have been petrified, but they were too trashed to care.

"Dan! Douglash! Mishter Cole!" they greeted us – myself, Douglas and Mr. Cole -- joyfully. "Whash happenin'?!" The three of us recoiled involuntarily, repelled by the alcohol waves rolling off each boy. Also none of us wanted to be a target when one of them puked, which seemed imminent given their age and level of inebriation.

Douglas, who served as head coach on this trip, was an Irish Catholic in his mid-20s. As a recent college graduate who was working as a bartender, he was more familiar with drunks than anyone at the Betty Ford Clinic. But he was also a soccer man through and through, a top player and as fierce a competitor as I've ever seen, and he knew this was not good preparation for the farewell game the following day.

Mr. Cole, the trip organizer and head parent chaperone, was a courtly Southerner. A high-powered businessman with three sons, he too knew his way around liquor. He seldom raised his voice, and this was no exception. He shot Douglas an I'll-take-care-of-this-later look, and simply told the boys: "Go home. Quiet down. Don't get in trouble.

We'll discuss this tomorrow."

Suddenly – or as suddenly as a drunken teenager's brain can process such things – the boys realized they were in trouble. "Shit," several of them said. "See ya," the one who was always the most polite mumbled. They lurched home. Fortunately, they were staying just a couple of streets away.

We retreated to the most logical place to discuss such an event – a beer garden – and were glad to see we all agreed. The boys would have to be punished with suspensions, for drunkenness and disorderly conduct. All five were starters; one was the goalkeeper. Clearly, this would hurt the team. For two long weeks, ever since Wollmatingen beat us in a closely contested opening match, then watched us improve game by game against teams from neighboring towns, both sides had primed for this final match. Though billed as a "friendly," everyone knew the winner would earn permanent transatlantic bragging rights.

The next afternoon the team assembled in an odd conglomeration of moods. A wonderful trip was nearing an end; the sadness of leaving melded with the anticipation of returning home to familiar food, individual bedrooms and shower heads you did not have to hold in one hand. The non-drinkers were just learning what had happened, and hustled off to the side for whispered consultations. The drinkers, whistling past the graveyard, talked too loudly about nothing.

Douglas, never one to pull punches, told the five miscreants to follow us into a side room. "Well, boys, you really fucked up last night," he began. Five eyes immediately looked down; they could tell by his tone that leniency was not an option.

"If I could, I'd put you on a plane back home right now," he continued. "But I can't. I'm stuck with you for another day. But you fucked yourselves as well as the team. You're not playing today. You're not even getting dressed. You're sitting in the stands. You're not going anywhere near the bench. Is that clear?"

Four of the boys nodded their heads. Two were crying. I thought they were sorry for all they had done: breaking team rules about drinking, making fools of themselves in public, letting the squad down. But then one asked, "Are you going to tell our parents?" and I realized their major concern was whether they would be in trouble when they got home too.

"I don't know," Douglas said curtly. "I'll leave that till later. Right now I don't give a fuck. I have a game to coach, and I have to figure out how to win it. Now get the hell out of here."

One boy – the fifth – finally spoke. "Douglas," he said. "I wasn't drunk. I was there, but I wasn't drinking."

Douglas, Mr. Cole and I were surprised. The night before he had seemed just as rowdy as the others; he was their friend, and we could not imagine this particular 14-year-old having the fortitude to sit in a bar and say, "No thanks, guys. I've got a game tomorrow, and besides, we're not supposed to be drinking. I'll just have sparkling water, *danke*."

We looked at the other four boys. Their eyes remained downcast. No one said a word. Their deafening silence spoke volumes. However, we could not convict a boy based on what his teammates did not say.

"Are you sure?" Douglas asked, giving him a chance to reconsider. "Because if I find out…."

"I swear, Douglas," he said. "I didn't drink. I swear to God."

"Okay, then," Douglas relented. "You play, they don't. Now all of you, get out of my sight."

The Wollmatingen crowd realized something was up, but were not sure what. When they saw the Westport Four trudge into the stands, wearing street clothes, they asked. Douglas described the previous night. Suddenly everyone began chattering in German. It was clear they were discussing what had happened. And although our German was limited to *bitte, guten tag* und *schnitzel*, it was also clear they disapproved.

"It is okay," the German coach said. "The boys are not bad. They can play." He seemed adrift in a sea of cultural misunderstanding. He thought his club had done something wrong, and wanted to avoid what he feared might be a major breach in German-American relations.

"They're not playing," Douglas said firmly. "They were out of control last night. They knew the rules."

"But it is okay to have a few beers once in a while, yes?" our host persisted.

"No," Douglas repeated. "No, it's not alright." And, undiplomatically but decisively, Douglas walked away.

The German coach shrugged. I knew he was remembering the many nights he had spent drinking with Douglas. *These Americans*, he must have thought. *What an odd bunch.*

On the field our four substitutes – including the reserve keeper – rose to the occasion. The game ended in a well-played, hard-fought draw. I did not look up in the stands very often, but I am sure our four suspended boys – being 14, embarrassed, angry and upset – hoped for two opposite outcomes: that we would not lose, so no one could say their absence hurt the team, and that we would get killed, so Douglas's decision would be seen as overly harsh. Their mood in the clubhouse after the match was primarily relief. The players who fought so hard to tie, meanwhile, felt tremendously proud of themselves. Dennis was happy that his hard line had been vindicated. The Germans admired his club for battling to a draw; he knew it, because they kept buying him beers.

As for our hosts, they added a graceful, even humorous note. At the final banquet, the German coach said, loudly enough for all to hear: "The American boys played very well tonight. So they should have beer, no?" Then he laughed heartily, indicating it was just a joke, *ja,* and announced: "Cokes for everyone!"

That put the proper end to the incident, I thought. Douglas had handled it forcefully yet fairly; now it was over, and everyone was eager to put it behind us. That is where it now lies, an interesting story we trot out whenever we reminisce about the past.

Yet for the four players who drank, and were punished, there is a postscript. They have long since graduated from college and scattered around the country. Their lives moved on; the trip to Konstanz has faded to a long-ago memory, relived at occasional weddings and reunions. The four realize now that Douglas's decision was just and fair. But even today, when they get together and discuss that night, they cannot believe that the fifth player lied, and let his friends take the rap. So they order another beer, and talk on and on about life as a kid.

And then there was Rick. His experience on that Konstanz trip was a bit different. He got the one thing teenagers want even more than beer. Rick got laid.

He was the one of the younger players in that group and, until that night, had not seemed unduly interested in the opposite sex. Many 14-year-olds talk a good game, but when confronted with a living, breathing female who shows an actual interest in them, realize they feel more comfortable playing a video game with their buddies. Rick was more the quiet type, which probably confirms the old saying that the guys who talk about it the most get it the least.

Perhaps it was that strong, silent characteristic that attracted Nina – the older sister of the boy who was hosting Rick – to him. Maybe it was his lopsided smile, or the glasses that made him look intelligent. Could be she just liked younger guys. Whatever it was, she slinked downstairs one night, put the moves on her prey, and faster than you can say "*Ach du lieber!*" Rick was no longer a virgin.

I found all this out after the fact, of course. Teenagers are not good at keeping secrets, but this one they managed to keep under cover, so to speak – at least until we got home. When I heard the story, it was told with a mixture of envy and awe. There was amazement, too, that it was Rick – not one of the self-styled studs -- who had done the deed.

In fact, the boys said, Rick was so unlikely a candidate for deflowering, he was unable to find the correct slang words when he spilled the beans as soon as he could, early the following morning. "I – I – I – I—I did it!" was all he managed to say. It was up to his older – and supposedly more worldly – teammates to pull the facts out of him, and realize the young soccer player had hit his first home run.

ARCHETYPES

I coached my first youth soccer team in 1975. For the first decade or so, I handled a couple of teams each spring. Then I came to my senses – I mean, I tapered off – to one. In the first falls there were junior high squads; then came high school freshmen, junior varsity and, now, varsity teams. That's probably 1,000 different players. But I feel like I've worked with only a few.

That's because the same boys show up again and again. Well, not the *same* ones – they'd be too old, and even worse they would know all my tricks – but the same *types*. Not every team has every one of the same kinds of players, of course, but enough do that I can make some generalizations. For example, nearly every team contains:

The Boy With Total Recall. He is the one who, when I mention a particular opponent – Redding, say – will erupt in a torrent of information. "Blue-and-gold uniforms. The first time we played them was up there, the field with the Port-a-Potty all the way in the woods. We won 3-1. Grant, Greer and Hulliman scored. Hulliman's was a PK. Way left – it hit the post and caromed in. Could have gone either way.

Dan, you were so pissed he went left, because he usually goes right. You told him if he couldn't be consistent with his penalties, you'd find someone else who was. Great burger joint on the way home. The second time we played them…" The scariest thing about The Boy With Total Recall is that he grows up to become The Man With Total Recall.

The Mathematician. The instant a match ends, The Mathematician can tell you what the result means. This talent is particularly valuable at tournaments, when he turns from his spot on the bench (The Mathematician is seldom The Starter), and says, "Dan, we don't need to score any more, but we have to keep our goals-against to finish first in our group. But, if we let up another goal, then we should probably let up three, because that would place us third overall, not second, and that would mean we would get to play Hamilton in the next round, and they're easier than Hicksville." Hearing a roar from the field behind us, he learns that Hamilton is at that very moment pulling off an upset. The Mathematician recalculates instantly, like an Excel spreadsheet in hyperdrive.

The Little Guy. Everyone has always told him he's too small to play; having had dozens of these players, I'm amazed at everyone's stupidity. The Little Guy is tougher than boys three times his size. He has blazing speed, boundless energy, great touch and no fear whatsoever. He has studied the game – often from the bench, because previous coaches favored bigger players over him – and his passion for soccer is boundless. His teammates look down at him physically, but up to him emotionally. No matter what his name is, he is always called Little Guy.

The Boy Who Does Things Differently. There are many variations of this archetype: the kid who rides a unicycle to practice when everyone else is chauffeured by mommy; the one who listens to classical music while the rest are into hip-hop; the soccer player who hangs out only with football players. But all Boys Who Do Things Differently are integral parts of their squads. Their teammates may not understand them, and they may be the center of curiosity, comments and jokes, but when the whistle blows they are as much a member of the team as anyone. And for some reason, they are the ones who grow up to have the strongest, most positive feelings for the time they spent playing soccer.

The Loner. A sadder version of The Boy Who Does Things Differently, The Loner is a soccer player who off the field hangs out with no one. He has no group of friends, either in the team or outside. As an adult who remembers how cruel teenagers can be, I try to make sure The Loner is included in group activities. But as an adult too, I know my ability to help him fit in is limited. Some loners, as they grew older, gain confidence and become comfortable in their own skin; others never do. The saddest loner I recall was the boy whose mother drove him to every game, because (I found out later) he was certain no one else would want him in their car. I never knew.

The Foreigner. I don't think I've ever had a team without one boy from another country. Their homelands vary – Holland, Germany, Brazil, Norway, Israel and India leap to mind – but the acceptance process seldom does. Initially wary at first, the youngsters open their arms the moment they see the newcomer can help. Their joking stereotypes – "Where are your wooden shoes?" "Does your mom drive a 'Fjord'?" "Have you ever headed a ball wearing a turban?" – help bring the new boy into the fold. Eager to fit in, the foreigner quickly becomes more American than the Americans. He wears a Duke baseball cap backward, picks up the slang of the day, and forgets his soccer shoes at home. Is this a great country or what?

The Captain Without the Title. Every team has a captain-wannabe. This is the boy who always must say something after the captain finishes his speech; who asks the coach what we're gonna work on today, and – unless I restrain him – would actually walk onto the field for the coin toss. The reason his teammates do not elect him captain is, of course, because he does all the things listed above.

The Musician. I have no idea why, but nearly every team I've ever coached has had at least one excellent musician. Drummers, guitarists, piano players, cellists, clarinetists – I've had them all. Sometimes The

Musician is happy to perform at a team social event; sometimes he doesn't want anyone to know he plays. I try to go to as many of The Musicians' concerts as I can, regardless of style. It gives me more insight into how well they perform under pressure.

Mr. Clueless. When God passed out brains, one player on each team was apparently wandering around on another field. Every year there is one boy with so little common sense, I fear for his safety in the real world. He is stupendously unable to arrive on time, hand in the proper forms and/or money, follow simple directions, or at times breathe unaided. Once he is on the soccer field, however, he often plays magnificently. This causes coaches to 1) tear their hair out and then 2) put him on the field in a very important position. Mr. Clueless often comes from an entire family of Cluelesses. It's a good bet that the reason he remains at the field long after dark is because his mother forgot he had practice – or does not know he is on a soccer team. In the most extreme case, his mother cannot even remember that she has a son.

The Soccer Expert. This player knows more about soccer at every level – club, high school, college, international, intergalactic – than Stephen Hawking knows about the universe. "Did you see the Djerdjukolozozovic-Brmdskji game on the Serbian sports channel?" he will burble. "What do you think North Dakota State-Minot's chances are in the NAIA women's tournament? Do you want to go with me on Saturday to see this awesome U-9 game?" Most of his teammates – who themselves are quite soccer-savvy – regard him with a mixture of awe and pity.

The Uniform Maven. A close cousin of The Soccer Expert, The Uniform Maven knows everything there is to know about jerseys, shorts, socks, shoes and balls. He is up on all the latest trends, both fashion ("Look at those stripes – there's five of them, not four, and check out the cool shade of black!") and function ("See, the new inner soles have compressed nitrous oxide, and there's a tiny layer of einsteinium that gives you more power"). I could care less what my team looks like, but the players do, so I find The Uniform Maven invaluable whenever I have to order anything. And he gets off on helping me no end.

The Perfectionist. Some boys take the coach's admonition "Do your best" to an unhealthy extreme. Nearly every year, I have one player who is never satisfied. We could win the most important championship, and he could score the only goal, but after the match he will focus on his one shot the keeper saved brilliantly. If we do not win, of course – or if we do, but he plays poorly – he transports himself beyond inconsolable, to another emotion so frightening words cannot describe it. Coaching The Perfectionist is very difficult, because by definition he lacks the most important quality any athlete needs: the ability to laugh at himself.

The Bad Boy. The Bad Boy can be bad for a number of reasons. He may test the coach's limits, by going beyond them. He may be every teacher's worst nightmare, spending more time out of class than in. He may be seeing three girls at once. He may be involved in drugs or alcohol. He may be doing all those things simultaneously. But for some reason, I seldom find The Bad Boy to be evil. Troubled, perhaps, and often caught up in a horrible home situation. A challenge, definitely. So – though it tests my sometimes limited amount of patience – I try not to let The Bad Boy make me mad. Instead, I do what I can to help. Sometimes I succeed. And when I do, I am strangely glad that I have this particular archetype on my team.

MORE TRAVEL TALES – PART II

I think of my European soccer trips the same way a mother looks at her children: She loves them all equally but differently, because each is unique. She would never choose a favorite, but with a gun at her head she might admit that one or two of her brood are certainly special.

That's how it is with me and the Warriors. This was a team I began coaching in the early 1980s. We stayed together for several years, for many reasons. They were a great team, and we had plenty of success. Their parents were overwhelmingly supportive, in that all-too-rare how-can-I-help way, not the what-can-I-do-and-by-the-way-I-expect-my-kid-to-be-the-star quid pro quo too common today. The players -- a highly competitive, highly motivated, high energy bunch -- formed ultra-tight bonds on and off the field. Their personalities shone more strongly as individuals, and meshed better together, than nearly any group I've ever seen.

Most importantly, they made me laugh.

We laughed through years of training and games. We laughed through state tournaments and regional competition. After we lost an amazingly tight match that would have sent our little town team on to the national level – we hit more wood than Ted Williams, one of our wits said – we cried, then laughed again a few minutes later. But we never laughed harder than during our 17 days in Iceland, Holland, Denmark and Sweden.

Nothing could keep the Warriors down. When life handed them lemons, they did not make lemonade – they prepared an entire picnic before you could say, "Aw, shit." A perfect example was the time Jake left his balls at the Hotel Absalon.

On every trip I make two assignments: the soccer balls and medical kit. Each player is assigned a day. I start at the top alphabetically with the balls – six or eight, tied in a mesh bag – and work down. I then start alphabetically at the bottom with the med kit, and work up. Some players luck out; if we're not playing or training, they don't have to lug the med kit anywhere. Others, however, must haul the balls onto buses, through airports and off luggage carousels. Whether a player gets a light or easy day is all chance. Hey, so is life.

Jake was one of those players I seem to have so many of: a tremendous athlete, scarily smart, less common sense than a tree toad. He could tell you anything you needed to know about the planet, but if you asked him where on earth he was, you'd just get a blank stare.

Our first stop had been Holland. We stayed in Zandvoort, a North Sea resort that had seen better days. It was cold, windswept and gray – typical July weather, I later learned. The boys did not care. They found the casinos, scoured the beaches for the topless bathers they were convinced were just over the next sand dune (in fact, there were no bathers at all, not even wrapped in blankets), and laughed uproariously at the windmill, cheese factory and wooden shoe store our guide dragged them to.

We had planned this two-day Holland sojourn as an acclimation to Europe, so there was no soccer. The boys reported they were "feeling soft," so halfway through our bus ride to Copenhagen we stopped at a rest area for a run. I asked Jake to lead them wherever he wanted. He could go forever; this would give the boys a good workout, while the two parent-chaperones and I relaxed with a nice meal.

Jake took them on a longer-than-forever run. Just when I started to get worried – I had forgotten to give him the crucial instructions, "Don't get lost!" – he came loping through the reeds. The team trailed several miles behind, but the mission was accomplished. They no longer felt soft, and the adults enjoyed some much-needed time to ourselves.

Soon we were in Copenhagen. The soccer portion of the trip would begin two days later in Sweden, but the boys wanted to train and I thought it was a great idea. I asked the hotel owner if he knew of a nearby field. He thought a moment, then gave directions involving three bus transfers, and 150,000 Hans Christian Andersen fairy tale-like shortcuts and side trips.

Off we trudged: 16 Warriors in soccer gear, two parents and I. Spirits were high. The boys were eager to play, though their attention was diverted every time a good-looking Danish girl got on the bus, which was only every stop.

Finally we arrived at the park. The boys laced up their shoes, stretched, then looked for soccer balls to kick.

Uh oh.

"Whose day was it for the balls?" I asked.

"JAKE!" they screamed in union.

"JAKE!" I screamed by myself.

"Uh oh," Jake said.

Then he laughed. "Guess I forgot them!" he announced.

A lesser team would have been angry. Another squad might have turned on Jake, called him the airhead he already knew he was, then gotten flustered because their practice plans were shot. But these were the Warriors.

"Don't worry, Dan. We can buy some balls!" Jake suggested. It was not a bad idea. We were in a city, after all; the Danes love soccer, so there had to be a sporting goods store somewhere.

God created slush funds for times like these. I peeled off a wad of kroners, handed them to Jake and said, "Okay. Go. But buy the cheapest balls you can find. Don't spend any more than you have to."

Once again I forgot to tell him not to get lost. Once again he took more time than a girl getting ready for the prom. But once again he finally reappeared.

He had taken my advice to heart. He had indeed bought the cheapest balls he could find. Unfortunately, they were not soccer balls. They were beach balls. Perhaps Jake did not realize the difference.

His teammates could not believe it. "You're a fucking idiot" was the nicest comment, and that about summed it up. Yet the Warriors had that magical ability to turn lemons into lemon meringue pie, and within minutes they were banging beach balls all over the park. They laughed at themselves as they tried to adapt to this new, odd way of playing. They ragged on each other as shots flew high, wide and ugly. They had the time of their lives – and, like the athletes they were, they adapted. It did not take long before they were controlling erratic beach balls as easily as soccer balls. Soon they were dribbling, passing and shooting like stars. After a while they forget they were playing with beach balls. And by the end of the session, they had learned two valuable lessons.

One: If you're a soccer player, you can play anywhere, any time, with anything.

Two: Given a choice between Jake and a tree toad, choose the toad.

Happily, Jake redeemed himself a couple of years later. The Warriors, by then a U-16 team, won the Connecticut state championship and traveled to Niagara Falls, New York for the Eastern U.S. regional tournament. Over 100 boys and girls teams, ages 12 through 19, converged from a dozen states; every player spent every spare moment crossing into Canada where the food was better, the video games more exciting, and the slot machines more alluring than the main U.S. attraction (a wax museum). Guards on both sides of the pedestrian bridge were lax -- this was back in the prehistoric pre-2001 days -- so the kids began showing library and YMCA cards as proof of identity.

But one day there was a random check, and who should get snagged but one of our players – an Israeli citizen, with no photo ID. The agent, fantasizing about thwarting an international plot, grabbed young Dov by the back of the neck, shoved him into a holding area, and threatened to toss him in jail. I have a very funny photo of Dov, sitting forlornly beneath a large picture of – I swear this is true – Ronald Reagan, but at the time we all were worried.

When Jake heard Dov say that his passport was back at the hotel room, he rose to the occasion. "I'll get it!" he said brightly. "It's a mile and a half each way," I pointed out. "No problem, Dan!" said Jake. And off he ran. He returned less than half an hour later – we did have to remind him to take Dov's room key – whereupon the guards scrutinized his passport, deemed Dov no threat, and released him. When the Warriors get together many years later, two of their favorite stories are of the time Jake left his balls at the Hotel Absalom, and the day he saved Dov from "being deported."

Even with the Warriors, however, life was not all fun and games. They were the first team I ever took to the Gothia Cup, and back in those days the Swedes were a bit too open-minded for their own good. They sold tournament souvenirs in a huge open air market. T-shirts were spread on dozens of tables, with only one or two workers watching the wares.

It did not take long to realize this was not a smart setup. As much as I liked my players, they were 14 years old, and impulse control was not their strong suit. The only thing Gothia Cup officials had not done was stick a sign on every table saying, "Steal me!"

So I devised a plan. That afternoon, when the team was together, I made an announcement. "Guys," I said, "I've got some bad news. I was walking through the souvenir tent today, and I saw one of you take something. I'm not going to embarrass whoever it was publicly, but you know and I know that stealing is wrong. You just can't do it. So here's what I'll do. If you're the one, you've got until 11 tonight to talk to me.

We'll handle this privately. Okay?"

"What if no one does?" asked a future lawyer.

"We'll worry about that then," I said. "For now, there's a few hours to think about what went on." Obviously, I had thought it through already. I had not actually seen any player steal a T-shirt, but I knew them well. I had a gut feeling something was going on. If no one said anything, I'd simply say that I had heard from one of them, he was sorry, we were handling the situation together, and that would be the end of that. Either way – a confession or not – I knew my ultimate aims would be achieved: Sending a strong message against shoplifting, putting the fear of God in the players, and preventing future problems.

However, I could never have prepared myself for the next several hours. Over and over – before dinner, after dinner, on the way downtown, on the way home, in the bathroom – boys sidled up to me. "Dan," they would say, their lips quivering. "I'm sorry...I'm so stupid...I'll never do it again...please don't send me home...."

Then the tears flowed. As they sobbed, I asked them why they did it. Invariably it was because they thought it was cool, or someone dared them to, or they wanted a T-shirt but didn't have the money right then. Then I'd ask what they thought should happen to them. Being sent home was a major worry; so was telling their parents. All of them mentioned that their parents always told them not to steal, and now they realized their parents were right. Then they blubbered some more.

Together, we came up with plans. They would return the T-shirt the next day. They would apologize to the vendors, pay for the merchandise, and offer to work in the souvenir stand. The boys agreed that was fair. I also promised them I would not tell their parents – *unless* they did something else stupid during the rest of the trip or any time afterward, until they died. The boys thought that was less fair, because it gave me a hammer to hold over their heads for eternity, but they had to admit I was a genius.

I was not surprised when the first boy turned himself in; he was, after all, not the most trustworthy type. The second boy was more of a shock. I congratulated myself, though, for reeling in two fish when I had cast about for only one. When number three bawled to me, I was truly stunned. I had never expected this boy to do anything like that; besides, it meant I had three thieves on the team. By the time the count reached six – nearly half the squad – I felt a welter of emotions. I congratulated myself for my cleverness in flushing out this ring of juvenile delinquents, but I was aghast at was going on. I wondered how endemic the problem was in other teams I had coached, and in our school and town. I began questioning all of American teenage society, and wondered what effect this incident would have on U.S.-Swedish relations if word got out. Finally, I realized how tired I was after dealing with so many sobbing boys.

The next day I told the players that I appreciated hearing from those who had confessed to stealing. I described my disappointment that there were so many of them, and hoped there were not others who had not turned themselves in. I urged them to use this as a learning experience.

I also vowed to be more proactive in the future. Nowadays, I tell this story to teams before we leave the U.S. Players understand from the start that I know much of what goes on; that I mean business, and that they represent their families, team, town and country. They are on notice that they must look out for each other. Two times since then, boys have told me quietly that teammates were stealing items overseas.

I don't relate the whole story to them, of course – I leave out the initial deception. But a couple of years after the Warriors trip I was still their coach, and I told them the truth.

There was stunned silence. The boys realized I had caught six of them, based solely on instinct; I had never actually seen even one of them stealing.

One of the Warrior Six looked at me, his eyes wide with admiration. This was the moment I'd been waiting for. Older now, he would understand what I had done. He would realize that sometimes a man must lie to find the truth. He would thank me for teaching him a lifelong lesson, and pledge to try to do the same if he ever found himself in a similar situation. Mentally, I began preparing my "heck, that's what coaches are for..." speech.

"Dan," he said. "You're a shithead."

And then, because he was a Warrior, he laughed.

Over many years traveling abroad, our teams have been guests of a variety of clubs. Only once, however, were our European hosts Americans.

That odd situation occurred in Heidelberg one summer, when we were housed by American families at a U.S. Army base. That gave our players and me an opportunity to view Europe – and the United States – with an almost Alice-through-the-looking-glass perspective.

For one thing, it opened our eyes to the military. Westport is not exactly Fort Benning. Growing up as our players do, attending an elite high school in an affluent New England suburb, the Army is far off their radar screen. But Heidelberg's base was headquarters for many senior officers and NATO personnel, and they talked avidly about their work. Many had been stationed overseas for years. They loved the service, and enjoyed defending Europe in a historic time. They communicated that enthusiasm well, but we also discovered a broad diversity of opinions among them. I learned to my surprise – hey, I'm a child of the '60s – that "military intelligence" is not an oxymoron. And I was intrigued that our hosts' insights into the changing face of Europe were expressed far more clearly and sharply than any comments I'd heard in the States.

The Westport boys learned about the life of "Army brats," and found their hosts anything but bratty. The worldliness of these American teenagers overseas was alluring. Our players were awed at how easily the Army kids traversed the lovely but confusing city of Heidelberg. (They were particularly impressed that their hosts not only knew all the best clubs and discos, but got in and were served, no questions asked.)

Meanwhile, the adults on the base were grateful for the chance to host an American soccer team. They were concerned that their children were growing up with no real knowledge of their home country. The parents – shedding their roles as military men and women, and becoming moms and dads – hoped our boys would provide insights into teen life in America. I'm not sure that backward baseball caps and rap music were what the adults had in mind, but those were the type of cultural totems our boys passed on.

As for me, one of the oddest moments came the day my host took me for a spin. I felt totally disconcerted racing down the autobahn in an enormous Cadillac, listening as the Armed Forces Radio Network broadcast baseball scores, stock prices and Randy Travis.

But the most remarkable part of our stay in Germany involved, of all people, Czechs. The Army group was simultaneously hosting a team from Strakonice. In fact, the day we arrived the Americans on the base drove 10 hours round trip to fetch them. This was the first time the Czech boys and their coaches had ever ventured beyond what a few months earlier had been the Iron Curtain. Their economy being what it was, all they could bring as gifts was Budwar beer (the original Budweiser, which at 12 percent alcohol is not a bit like our Bud). Yet not until we saw their generic soccer shoes, shorts and other paraphernalia did we realize the width of the gap between even as relatively advanced a country as Czechoslovakia, and the West.

Another eye-opening experience came when a Czech coach told me, "You are the first American I have met since our revolution. Have you heard of it?"

Had I heard of it?! "The whole world was excited," I said. "You must be so excited that Havel has brought democracy to your country."

The man beamed. "Good!" he said. "I was hoping you knew of it."

On our final day in Heidelberg the Czechs gave us pins from their town – with an American flag prominently displayed. The reason, they proudly explained, was that although U.S. troops liberated Strakonice at the end of World War II, for 40 years the Soviets told them their saviors were Russian soldiers wearing American uniforms. When the Czechs learned the truth, they added the Stars and Stripes to their town seal.

Witnessing all that on a U.S. Army base was mind-boggling. It illustrated more graphically than any newspaper article or television report the speed with which the world was changing. And while on the one hand I hoped our players appreciated the experience, on the other I wished that someday soon they would wonder what all that East-West fuss had been about.

Dachau is no one's idea of a vacation spot. But for four days 15 players, my assistant coach Jerry and I lived there, just a few miles away from the first Nazi concentration camp. We went with a certain amount of trepidation, and – as often happens on these trips, though usually in less fraught places than Dachau – returned home with impressions far different from those we had expected.

Dachau would not have been my first – or even last – choice for a vacation destination. But I was not the one choosing. For over two decades my trips were organized by Euro-Sportring, a non-profit organization that arranged travel, tournaments, training sessions and home stays for soccer (and other sports) teams. My working and personal relationships with their personnel were excellent. Each trip turned out spectacularly; the arrangements were virtually flawless. I trusted Euro-Sportring's judgment, because I knew they had my and my team's best interests at heart.

So when we agreed to a home stay in "the Munich area," I never thought to request "no former concentration camps, please." Besides, although I had of course heard the horrible tales of Dachau, I had no idea it was still a functioning town. Or that it was anywhere near Munich.

Three weeks before we were to leave, I received our final itinerary. When I examined our home stay arrangements, my heart skipped several beats. Our genial hosts lived in Dachau.

As luck would have it, several players on that squad – as well as Jerry, the assistant coach – were Jewish. I am too, by birth, although I no longer practice my faith. ("So how come you always tell us how important it is to practice?" a player once asked slyly.) Most of the Jewish players and Jerry were, like me, fairly lackadaisical Jews. Yet they had been bar mitzvahed, and their parents belonged to the local temple.

I put off uttering the "D" word as long as I could. Finally, when I handed out all the contact information, the team learned we would be staying in Dachau. I assured the parents that I had spoken to the German coaches and club leaders, and all were well aware of American sensitivities. They promised me that the Dachau of the late 20th century was nothing like 50 years earlier, and I conveyed those assurances to our mothers and fathers. Nevertheless, I could not help wondering if any of the people we would meet were among those who, 50 years earlier, gave Dachau such a dastardly name.

Our boys – even the Jewish ones -- were much less concerned than their parents. For them, Dachau does not conjure up the images it does for adults around the globe. And it was obvious – in subtle, unspoken but nonetheless clear ways – that the men and women who hosted us were acutely aware of their town's reputation. They told us, mirroring some of the unease I felt, that in all their years working with Euro-Sportring, this was the first time they ever welcomed an American group. Left unsaid was their desire to prove it could be done.

The first thing they showed us, the morning after we arrived, was the concentration camp. For two hours the Westport teenagers, accompanied by several of the boys they stayed with, wandered through the exhibits. We toured the barracks and crematoria, and watched a film. There was none of the joking, milling around, glazed looks or searches for souvenirs and sodas that usually fills adolescents' trips to historic sites. They were as silent as I'd ever seen a group of soccer players. When they spoke, it was to ask a question they truly wanted answered.

The experience was both important and sobering. It was infinitely more valuable than reading a book about Nazis, watching a video or hearing a lecture.

Those two hours were the right amount of time. Our morning at the concentration camp left a life-long impression. But youth must always look forward, and for the rest of our visit the boys learned about modern Germany. Many of their hosts – at 15 and 16, the same age as the American boys – were already working full-time. Our players realized how different the European education system is from ours. Yet that did not prevent both groups from becoming friends, as teenagers around the world do so easily. Each night they headed off together to discos, cafes and other areas of mutual interest.

One night we all attended the Altstadtfest, a townwide Okotberfest-like blowout featuring singing, eating and hilarious quantities of beer. Our players found it remarkable that entire extended families sat convivially together, enjoying each other's company, even dancing together. "At home I spend all my time figuring out how to avoid my parents," one said. An intriguing discussion of family values, American-style, followed.

Twice our Dachau hosts took us into nearby Munich. Our boys reciprocated by organizing a three-on-three basketball tournament, combining American and German players. It was funny – and instructive – to see the German version of that sport. While they played adequately, it was clear they had worked to learn the sport. They had not grown up with it – just as our players did not grow up in a soccer culture.

Every day the boys raved about German hospitality. One mother ironed a player's underwear; another gave him a pair of sneakers because she thought his were too worn. (The unlaced-is-cool concept had not yet crossed the Atlantic.) In fact, several days after we left Dachau for Italy, a boy confronting a reeking pile of jerseys, shorts and socks asked, "Do I really have to wash these? In Germany I just put them on the floor, and the next morning they were on my bed, folded."

Not until we returned to the United States did I realize the high level of anxiety some of the Jewish parents felt about our Dachau sojourn. I had not been aware of the phone calls they traded, or the anguished emotions they felt letting their sons head off to a place that held such horrible connotations.

I was glad I had not been privy to all that pre-trip angst. I was happy that, in phone calls when they were away and long conversations when they came back, the players assuaged their parents' fears. But what pleased me most was that the parents did more than listen to their sons' stories, and glance at their photos. They actually heard and saw what their boys had gone through. And they understood.

Judaism is a religion that places an enormous emphasis on tradition, and passing down important truths from one generation to the next. This time, the youngsters taught their elders a vital lesson. The boys had confronted an ugly past. They would certainly never forget it.

But, on the other hand, they would never let it enslave them.

MANNY'S ORPHANS

I admit it: "Manny's Orphans" is not a particularly memorable movie. "Rocky," "Rambo" or "Raiders" it ain't.

But cable TV has created an insatiable demand for movies of any type of quality, and "Manny's Orphans" – a full-length feature film telling the hopelessly clichéd story of a team of soccer-playing orphans, their girl goalie and high-living coach as they face their prep school archrivals in The Big Game (you'll never believe it, but the orphans win!) – fills the bill.

It was filmed in my back yard – Fairfield County, Connecticut – and I had a hand and foot in it. I served as "soccer adviser" (that's what the credits say), along with a minor screen role as the referee. "Manny's Orphans" crops up every few months on cable these days. It's not on in prime time, of course; more like 6 a.m. Sunday mornings. It has migrated downward from HBO and Showtime, through The Movie Channel and TNT (missing, for some reason, American Movie Classics), all the way down to Joe-Bob's Cable Network, which if you subscribe to your provider's Glutton Plan can be found on Channel 2835. Somehow – and this does not bode well for America's future -- nearly every boy I ever coached has managed to see it. I do not ask why they watch obscure television stations in the pre-dawn darkness, but every time a player says incredulously, "Hey, Dan, I saw your movie on TV!" I am transported back to the summer I spent on the set of "Manny's Orphans."

I received my baptism in moviemaking the very first day of shooting. Director Sean Cunningham – who got his start in porn, made a pit stop for quasi-respectability with "Manny's Orphans" and the equally unmemorable "Here Come the Tigers" (a blatant ripoff of "Bad News Bears," but with more swear words), then zoomed on to far greater fame and success producing "Friday the 13th" and "Spring Break" – asked me to lay out a soccer field in the rock-strewn Bridgeport park that would serve as the orphans' "home field." Carefully, I paced off the dimensions: the penalty area here, 44 yards across and 18 yards deep; the midfield stripe there, including a center circle with a radius of 10 yards; even a corner kick arc. A group of flunkies followed dutifully behind, laying down lines just crooked enough to look real, and marking all my commandments in a spiral notebook for future reference.

It was a perfect soccer field, just what the orphans needed for their movie debut. Proudly, I knocked on Sean's trailer door. He was busy doing what directors do, which is swearing at someone because something somewhere has gone wrong. "Field's done!" I chirped.

He stepped out to look. "What the fuck is that?" he sputtered.

"The field!" I said proudly.

"It's too goddamn big," he said. "Make it smaller." He headed back to his trailer, then turned around again. "Much fucking smaller," he clarified.

By early afternoon our field was done. It certainly was much fucking smaller. In fact, it was so small you could barely fit four players on it. That, I learned, was the idea. Sean could only film three or four players at a time. This was a movie, after all; it was not a fucking soccer game.

Fueled by a catered lunch – hey, it might be downtown Bridgeport, but this was a *movie set* – Sean and I devised a few simple scenes. I had recruited the players – most were 13 and 14 years old, playing on the team I coached – so that part was easy. Each scene involved one or two crisp passes, ending with a shot on goal. We strove for action, grace and skill. The choreography was gorgeous in rehearsal, and we loved what we saw. The boys practiced over and over again until they got it right.

Once the cameras finally rolled, what they got was an epidemic of stage fright. Balls flew in every direction except the right one. Boys tripped over each other like the Three Stooges, and called each other by their given -- not their film -- names.

They soon conquered their jitters and felt at ease with cameras trained on them. Almost immediately, though, they tilted in the opposite direction. They relaxed too much, and started directing the film themselves. Each one wanted to be the star; each found a way to maneuver himself smack in front of the camera, no matter where Sean or I positioned him.

Luckily Sean, who had a son the same age, demonstrated a special talent for working with children. "Cut the fucking shit," he said eloquently. "You'll go where Dan and I tell you to go, or you won't go any fucking where at all."

Throughout the long, hot afternoon scenes were created, rehearsed, scrapped, reworked and finally filmed. At one point everything came together, like movie magic. The lighting was just right, the background clean, the sound men poised for action. Hurriedly, Sean looked around for the soccer players. Okay, he screamed for them.

They were off in a remote corner, engrossed in a show presented by a young production assistant. She was demonstrating a yoga exercise, contorting her stomach muscles like a pretzel. By the time she was back to normal the light had changed, a train chugged through the background, and the sound men wanted a cigarette break.

"Fuck this shit," said Sean.

Back on the set, frustration mounted. Cues were blown, passes missed and tempers flared. Some of the boys – excellent players all – found it physically impossible to make a bad pass on purpose. Others found it embarrassing to act dorky, or fall down while attempting to trap the ball. They seemed to believe the film would be seen by dozens of European coaches, all of whom would think the boys could not play soccer if they made a bad play in a movie, and thus would not offer them professional contracts.

Mercifully, Sean called for a break. A player raced over to a long-haired cameraman and relayed a message: The cast challenged the crew to a pickup soccer game.

"Eat shit," replied the cameraman, leaving no doubt as to his feelings about the proposed match, all the young actors and the sport of soccer in general.

Undaunted, the boys sped off. At the far end of the park they discovered a pack of girls, shyly watching the filming. Some, who looked at least three or four years older than the boys – in adolescent terms that translates into centuries – asked for autographs. "To the prettiest girl in Bridgeport," wrote one mack daddy-wannabe.

The girls wanted to know what their heroes were being paid. "Well, we just got back from Rome, and we got $500 a day there," one lied grandly. The others nodded wisely. The girls swooned.

Soon, however, filming grew routine. Over the next two months, as the youngsters acted more professional and businesslike, the pace accelerated. They learned about camera angles, voice levels and makeup. They also learned how to hurry up and wait.

So they created their own diversions. One soccer game the boys invented was called, for lack of a better name, "See How Close You Can Come to the Camera Without Actually Hitting It." The game ended abruptly one morning when a player – allegedly quite by accident – miskicked the ball and slammed it off the top of the most elaborate camera, nearly toppling it from its very sturdy tripod. Every adult on the set panicked, while the kicker grinned sheepishly.

Another memorable moment occurred the day the Panaglide arrived. This camera rested on a system of springs, allowing the operator to balance it on his shoulder while running amid the action. It was a technological marvel, perfect for a film such as ours. It was also heavy as hell, and cost $600 an hour to rent. The latter fact impressed our young actors so much that the Panaglide was deemed exempt from the kicking game.

Virtually every story from that summer involves cameras, in some way, shape or form. One day a boy complained because the camera batteries, which lasted eight minutes each, had to be changed so often.

"Stop bitching," Sean soothed. "In your spare time, why don't you invent a better fucking one."

All summer long I yelled at the players for blowing their lines, being unprepared and missing their marks (the spots to end up at for the desired camera angles). Finally it was time to film my big referee's scene. I rehearsed diligently: I ran, tooted my whistle, faced the camera and said, "No! That's a foul!" (No referee would actually utter those words, of course, but who was I to dispute writer Steve Miner? His dialogue was actually pretty funny – and "Manny's Orphans" was just a prelude to his greater success on such televisions shows as "The Wonder Years" and "Dawson's Creek.")

Sean yelled, "Shoot!" I ran. I tooted my whistle. I faced the camera. I said my lines clearly, loudly, flawlessly.

Sean yelled, "Cut!" I stood there and smiled. I was a star.

Sean walked over. He looked at me, up and down. "Dan," he said quietly, "we have to do it again. You missed your mark."

Near the end of the filming, when the boys had grown positively blasé about the whole affair, we shot some crowd scenes at a local private school. Notices were placed in the local newspaper. Dozens of townspeople appeared, lured by the prospect of a silver dollar for a day's work and a lifetime of immortality. We knew it was a big event, because two portable toilets were trucked in to serve the masses.

Because it was a Saturday, many of the soccer players' families were on the set for the first time. It was amusing to see the youngsters so calm and collected, while their parents jockeyed for the best camera angles. A few weeks earlier, their sons had done exactly the same thing.

The boys were rewarded for their hard work and perseverance a few days later. One of the final scenes was a gigantic food fight between the orphans and the preppies, held during a dance before The Big Game. It was shot inside the private school library, as ornate a place as one would expect a Fairfield County private school library to be. Paintings were covered with invisible protective coating; valuable globes were removed, and expensive tables and chairs were replaced by inexpensive (but expensive-looking) substitutes. Caterers carted in enough doughnuts, cookies and bowls of punch to feed several debutante balls.

There could be only one take; there would not even be a practice run. The boys had to get it right the first time. Sean told them all they need to know: "Have a great food fight. Do whatever you want to do. But don't fuck up the cameras, and don't fuck up yourselves."

The cameramen, the sound men and all the hangers-on were ready. Sean yelled "Shoot!" Instantly, the boys went to town.

Food flew everywhere. Brownies got smushed into faces. Punch bowls were upended on tops of heads. One boy picked up an entire cake, held it out while racing toward a camera, then veered away at the final second. For several minutes the staid library was absolute mayhem. Then Sean yelled, "Cut!" The boys – by now professional actors – stopped.

They stood stock still, viewing the carnage all around them. Jelly dripped from the ceiling. Pies squished underfoot on the fake-expensive carpeting, and soda matted everyone's hair. They had just had the mother of all food fights – and gotten paid for it. It was every boy's wet dream.

Sean looked around. His actors had had one take, and they nailed it. For once, he broke into a smile.

"Nice job, boys," he praised. "Nice fucking job."

Filming ended in late August, with a special scene at Giants Stadium (the film's protagonist hitchhikes there to find his hero, Cosmos captain Werner Roth. Hey, it was the '70s.) When a sneak preview was held months later in Westport, the results were predictable. Many members of the capacity crowd – including me – eagerly awaited their film debuts.

There were a few isolated yelps of recognition, but we soon settled back to enjoy what was, in the words of one critic (me), "a well-paced, fairly funny – and, to be honest, a trifle trite" – film. The audience reacted just as it would have had the actors been a bunch of strangers. (Most of the time, anyway. A gaggle of eighth-grade girls did giggle when they saw their friends, larger than life on the movie screen, wearing only underwear.)

But "Manny's Orphans" never returned to Westport for a regular run, so it was no surprise that it sank in the rest of the country without so much as a ripple. I'm not even sure it made it onto airplanes, where similar films go to die. Sean soon discovered he could make more money in ax murderers and nubile 20-year-olds than in adolescent soccer players, and forsook Connecticut for California.

Yet cable TV has given "Manny's Orphans" a new life – an overtime period, if you will. I heartily recommend that every soccer fan in America seek it out, at whatever odd time it's being shown. I still watch it occasionally – a fact made easier several years ago when I found it in the used bin of a dusty independent video store.

Although no one beyond my pre-dawn-viewing soccer players has ever heard of it, there are certain moments I am convinced should live forever in film history, such as the food fight, the referee's scenes, and of course the ending.

That's when the credits – specifically, my credit – roll elegantly across the screen.

MARTIN

One of the first coaching lessons I learned is that lack of common sense has nothing to do with lack of brains. Over the years I worked with googols of bright young men who, practically speaking, were a few peas short of a casserole. Martin was among the very brightest, and yet most common sense-impaired, of all these young men. His interests ranged from astrophysics to Zen philosophy. With so much going on in his mind, I suppose he had little time for such mundane ideas as what time it was, where he was supposed to be, or what he should do when he got there.

This could have been a genetic trait – Martin was often the last boy picked up from practice, and we're talking wait-until-dark late – but I didn't realize how bad things were until our European trip. We spent the first few days in Maastricht, the oldest city in Holland. It's a beautiful place, right down by the borders with Belgium and Germany. We stayed at a sports training center a few kilometers away. It had a long, guttural name, which the players referred to by clearing their throat and spitting. But I felt it was important they know where they were in case they got lost – not that they dared to – so I made them memorize a portion of it: Duisberg. In Dutch it sounds like "Dweesberg," with lots of rollings of the tongue and phlegmish noises, but as Americans we pronounced it "Doosberg."

Because I think that soccer trips should involve much more than soccer – a heretical notion, believe it or not, when you see all those American teams in Europe who train three times a day, live in hotels, obey an 8 p.m. curfew, and whose entire cultural experience is limited to one hour at a windmill, castle or soccer store – I make sure whenever I'm in the greater Maastricht area to stop at an American military cemetery not far from the city. It is a stunning site: row after row of gleaming white headstones, all perfectly aligned, honoring thousands of U.S. soldiers who died in the final days of World War II.

There are so many lessons to learn here. The headstones

themselves -- most decorated with crosses, some with Stars of David, a few with crescents – along with the movie-like ethnic stew of names tell a powerful tale of America's diverse society. A few graves serve as the final resting places of men who succumbed to wounds in May and June 1945, weeks after the war in Europe ended. I always point that out, and note that many of the soldiers were just two or three years older than our boys are now. The fresh-mown grass and immaculate landscaping serve as mute testimony to the debt the Dutch feel to their American friends, more than half a century later. And an enormous wall map, filled with nearly incomprehensible arrows and lines and symbols, demonstrates far better than any history teacher ever could the horrors that befell this lovely land not once but twice, when the players' grandparents and great-grandparents were young.

Martin, who loved history as well as science and math, took it all in. But eventually it was time to move on, so I shepherded the players to the bus. We were ready to head through rolling countryside to our next stop, 30 minutes away: a quaint Dutch village filled with outdoor cafes and wooden shoe stores. Hey, these kids can never have enough culture.

Before leaving, I went through my drill. I strolled down the aisle, physically counting heads. One, two, three...fourteen, plus one assistant coach. I nodded to the driver: *Roll 'em!*

Along the way, I did paperwork. The players did what they always do on a bus: listened to music, talked, slept, asked how much longer it would be.

When we got to the quaint Dutch village, one of the boys asked, "Dan, where's Martin?"

"What do you mean?" We had just gotten off the bus; even someone as spacey as he could not have gotten lost that soon.

"He wasn't on the bus."

"Of course he was," I said. And, when I looked around, I realized the truth: Of course he wasn't.

"But I counted," I said, hoping that statement would make Martin materialize out of thin air.

"Yeah, I think you counted the guide," a player suggested helpfully.

I am not a big fan of swearing, but my players are; in fact, the first foreign words they learn are swears. (It's a cultural exchange thing; in return they help young foreign players learn the latest English lingo.) So I said something like "Farfigneuven" that I'd just picked up, and realized I had, in fact, counted our guide. Hell, her hair was short, and she had been sitting with her head down. Anyone would have made that mistake.

So I did the only thing I could: I left my assistant coach with the 13 boys, told the driver what happened, and went back through the rolling countryside to the cemetery. It was a lot less interesting the second time around.

Along the way, I wondered how to react. Should I yell at Martin for not having gone to the bus when I asked, or apologize because, after all, I was the one who miscounted? Should I punish him, because a 15-year-old should keep better track of time and his surroundings, or would that be blaming a kid for the mistake of an adult? And I wondered something else: What if I couldn't find Martin? What if he'd taken matters into his own hands and tried to meet up with us – though all he knew was that we were headed toward "a quaint Dutch village"? Or what if he had simply disappeared?

As the bus turned into the long entrance, I noticed a taxi cab ahead. How odd – who would take a taxi to or from a cemetery? Then it hit me: Martin had called the cab. How clever. How resourceful. How bad it would be if he had gone off in the taxi, and I had not had any idea where he was.

But there he was, standing on the curb as the taxi and bus pulled in together. He waved happily to me, then spoke to the taxi driver. After an animated conversation, he returned to the bus.

"Where'd you guys go?" he asked.

"To the stupid quaint Dutch village, just like I said," I said. "Where the farfigneuven were you?"

"I was just looking at the maps," he said. "They're so cool. Have you seen them? Did you know…" And on and on he went, giving me a mini-history lesson. Meanwhile, I wanted to give him a smack upside the head.

But I was sure that was against Dutch law – they are a very child-oriented people – so instead I talked.

"That was a good idea to call a taxi," I said magnanimously. "But where were you going to go?"

"Duisberg," he said. "But there was something really weird with that taxi driver. He said it was like 100 miles away in Germany, and I wasn't sure I had enough money. We're not staying in Germany, are we?"

That's when I realized I had arrived in just enough time to avert a true disaster. Martin's American accent – and lack of specificity that he was staying at the "Dweesberg" Sports Center near Maastricht – would have sent him to a large German city of the same name, pronounced "Doosberg." And Martin – who might have understood the theory of relativity better than I, but who nevertheless had trouble keeping track of time here on earth – might never have realized he was in a different country than the rest of his team.

Several days later we were all in Germany. We were hosted by a team in Dachau – quite an experience for our group, which included several Jewish boys. The first morning, our hosts took us to the concentration camp, a sobering experience for everyone. They then spent the next several days proving that the Dachau of the 1990s was not the same place it was a half century earlier.

The Dachau parents and players were friendly and outgoing, befitting their Bavarian heritage, and were eager to show off the nearby city of Munich. They were especially proud of the Olympic village, site of the 1972 Israeli massacre – er, the 1972 Olympics.

The main stadium – where the 1974 World Cup was also held – was particularly noteworthy. The grass was green, the stands impressive, the signs warning everyone that straying onto the field was STRICTLY VERBOTEN clear and bold.

So imagine my surprise, 10 minutes into our tour, when I saw Martin and a teammate – a quiet, shy boy who has since earned a degree in comparative religions – being escorted up the stairs by a pair of exceptionally stern-looking *polizei*. This being Germany, they toted machine guns. It was our lucky day; the men still pointed them skyward.

I did not want to ask, but I had to. "Dan, all we did was go on the grass! I didn't know what the sign meant. It was in German!" Those were Martin's last words, before being unceremoniously tossed out of the stadium. I could tell by his eyes that he did not think he had done anything wrong. However, he understood that being booted by the German police was not a good career move, coming as it did just a few days after being left at a Dutch cemetery.

His teammates, meanwhile, wanted to laugh, but figured – and they might not have been far off the mark – that provoking grim-looking men with machine guns, and an equally grim-looking American soccer coach, was not the wisest course of action. As for our Dachau hosts, they were simply horrified. A Teutonic primal fear of consequences was kicking in, I think.

At any rate, Martin's ouster was a definite buzzkill. Our trip to the

Olympic site was over; we headed off to a technology museum, which most of the players hated. Except Martin, of course; he wandered happily through the halls. It bothered him not a bit that all the exhibit explanations were in German; he was more interested in going off alone and figuring out how everything worked. To his credit, he showed up well before it was time to leave. His teammates, who had spent most of their time in the museum's cafeteria, were delighted to get back to Dachau and party.

As for Martin, several years later I asked him to be my assistant coach. We would shepherd another group of young players to Europe – including Maastricht, the American military cemetery and Dweesberg, Doosberg or however the farfigneuven you pronounce it.

Sometime between the moment I asked him to help coach and our departure, Martin popped the question. Why, he wondered, had I chosen him – among all the other former players – to be my assistant? He knew he had the soccer talent, and worked well with younger kids. But what about being left behind at the cemetery? And getting tossed out of the stadium in Munich?

Those were good questions, and I knew I had to answer him honestly. "Martin," I said looking him in the eye. "To tell you the truth, I forgot."

DEATH COMES QUICKLY -- PART II

Soccer has been described – accurately – as a safe sport. Virtually every injury I have seen has been minor: sprains, strains, contusions, concussions. So when a 13-year-old boy playing for the Westport Soccer Association – the organization I helped found – died in a freak accident, faith in the game as a fun, wonderful and harmless diversion was shaken to its core.

Michael was a youngster any parent would want as a son: outgoing, witty, popular, interested in all sports, a member of his middle school honor society. He was a reserve goalkeeper on the local travel team, a perennial state power.

One Sunday in mid-November his team faced a neighboring town in the season's final match. The outcome would determine the U-13 champion of Connecticut's Southwest District.

At halftime Westport's starting keeper asked to come out. He had hurt his hand earlier, and it bothered him. Michael warmed up, and started the second half.

Midway through, with his team down 3-2, Michael stopped an initial shot, then went for the rebound. At that moment an opponent knocked into him, shoulder to shoulder. The contact was not bruising, but neither was it fierce. A father said later, "I've seen hundreds of games, and thousands of worse collisions. This wasn't anything to get excited about."

But Michael did not get up.

When it was apparent that his injury was severe, many people swung into action. His mouth was pried open, because at first it appeared he had swallowed his tongue. A dentist began CPR. One man raced across the street to call for help; another drove to a nearby nursing home to see if medical personnel were available.

Michael's dad was at the game. Michael's mom, a flight attendant, was in Boston, about to board a flight to Europe. A father on the other team with a private plane immediately flew two Westport parents to Boston, to bring her home.

Michael's heart continued to beat for a while. For two hours doctors worked on him, at the field and in the hospital. But essentially he was dead before he hit the ground.

The cause of death, as determined by the state medical examiner the next day, was "a whiplash-type injury" that severed the carotid artery, causing a brain hemorrhage. There are two carotid arteries, one on either side of the neck. Both are nearly always protected. But for one split second that day, because of the position of Michael's neck, the artery was vulnerable. At that instant, it was hit.

It happened in a soccer match, so in that sense it was a soccer injury. But it could also have happened in a baseball game or a pillow fight. Of course, how it happened was irrelevant. The irreversible fact was that a 13-year-old boy was dead.

The next several days were terrible. The players had to deal with watching a teammate and friend die in front of their eyes. Everyone harbored "what if" feelings. Michael's best friend, a defender, felt guilty for not clearing the ball. The starting goalkeeper felt guilty for having asked to come out of the game. The teenage referee was filled with remorse. The player on the other squad who ran into Michael was particularly devastated. Michael's mother, in a brave and compassionate gesture, called him personally the day of the funeral, and begged him not to blame himself.

Plenty of adults, though grief-stricken themselves, mobilized to help the youngsters. Crisis teams in the Westport schools – organized in response to previous tragedies – met Sunday night and Monday morning. One of Michael's first coaches opened his home to all. For three days the house was jammed with boys. They ached to talk, or simply be together. The former coach met with the players in small groups. He explained, thoroughly and clearly, exactly how Michael died. He stressed how remotely it was related to soccer. Answering all the "what ifs," he said to one boy, "What if Michael hadn't started playing goalie for me six years ago? You just can't think like that."

Michael's funeral was held on a Wednesday. Every seat was filled, and 150 people stood in back. The service was almost too much to bear, but in a way it was cathartic. In one particularly touching moment, Michael's closest friend tenderly shook the hands of players from the opposing team, who sat nearby.

Later in the week a parent took the boys to a New York Islanders game. He arranged for them to meet Mike Bossy, a personal friend. The hockey star spoke eloquently and honestly of the tragedies he had endured, and described how he recovered from them. The youngsters' spirits rose, almost visibly.

On the following Sunday, just one week after Michael's death, the coaches arranged a pickup game. They wanted to make sure the players did not spend all winter thinking of the soccer field as a place of death and anguish. They and several other parents played too. It was a rewarding and important afternoon. For the first time in a while, the boys laughed.

In the aftermath of the tragedy, I was asked repeatedly whether soccer is truly as safe as it seems. I said yes. It is a sport – especially at the youth level – of skill and fitness. Most youngsters – certainly those on Michael's team, and his opponents that day – were taught to play hard, but fairly. The object, they knew, was to get the ball, not the man. The emphasis on techniques and tactics, plus the fact that soccer players run so much that they are in strong physical shape, makes it safe for youngsters, and attractive to them.

A neurosurgeon was quoted in a local newspaper as saying that soccer is so dangerous, he does not know any doctor who lets his child play. I had never heard such a thing before. Other people called for the introduction of helmets.

Shin guards do help. I have seen several potential broken legs averted by guards, and I believe their use should be mandatory at all levels.

In addition, every league should require all coaches and referees to take first aid, sports medicine and physiology courses. All coaches should know (and teach) proper warm-up and stretching techniques, including neck exercises. Every coach must carry a cell phone, at all times. Thanks to my high school booster club, I now have an AED (portable electronic defibrillator).

Unfortunately, none of those measures would have saved Michael's life. As one doctor said, "Even if this had happened inside a hospital, we couldn't have saved him."

Michael died in a freak accident, while playing soccer. The game is strong, and it survived. The players were strong, too, and young and resilient. They continued to play. They loved the game, and achieved a great deal of success in high school. Several went on to play in college. Two continued professionally.

But for the rest of their lives, they missed a teammate and friend. And all of their joy could not erase the tragedy of Michael's death, or make it any easier to bear.

The call was as unexpected as it was horrifying: Dick had died.

Of all the parents of players I have coached, he was the last I would expect to go. In his mid-50s, trim, vigorous, a banker and honors graduate of Yale University who involved himself in a million projects, ranging from the symphony to a home for the elderly, Dick epitomized the concerned, active citizen. And of course there was soccer...

Driving the three miles to his house, thoughts of Dick and soccer tumbled through my mind. I'd first met him more than a decade ago, when I coached his son David. He was a goalie – but at 12 David decided there was more to the game than standing in front of a net his teammates guarded more than adequately.

After the season, Dick called. In my coaching career I have heard from many discontented parents, most of whom figure the louder and more belligerently they talk, the better, but Dick's approach was different. Calmly, quietly and persuasively, he made the case that David would be happier – and the team better – if he were allowed to try the field.

I agreed. It turned out to be a great move – and Dick never stopped thanking me for it. In truth, I should have thanked him.

Over the next several years I bonded more tightly with that team than nearly any other I've coached. There were hills and valleys, of course, but overall that ride was among the most fun and memorable of all. And that's saying something.

I remembered so much as I neared the house. There was the year we won the state championship, and qualified for the U.S. Youth Soccer Association regional tournament in Niagara Falls. Unasked, Dick made all the travel arrangements – and convinced virtually all the parents to go. They had a marvelous time: 30 men and women packing up on a few days' notice, laughing and eating and enjoying their kids, with soccer the common bond.

When we planned our European trip Dick leaped in with all the enthusiasm of a player, even though he remained in the States and experienced our adventure only vicariously. It was, I think, the only time he did not see David play. Tuesday afternoon or Sunday morning, indoor or outdoor, championship match or preseason scrimmage, Dick was there. Win or lose, he was always cheering, always excited – and always cared as much for the game and all 22 players on the field as he did for his own son.

The year after Europe, we reciprocated. The final day of the Swedes' visit, we assembled for a fun game. We mixed both teams together. Soon the Swedish fathers joined in, laughing and gleeful. They urged the American men to do the same, but most of our parents remained on the sideline. They'd never kicked a ball, and did not want to look foolish.

Except for Dick. He raced onto the field, and soon banged goal kicks far beyond the center stripe. Only later did I learn he'd actually played soccer as a youngster; he just never told anyone. It seemed I was always learning something about him.

My mind flashed forward to David's senior year in high school. The season-ending banquet was a wonderful affair. As emcee, I was about to deliver closing remarks when Dick approached the head table, and asked to say a few words.

With no idea what was coming, I handed him the mike. He faced the audience, and in 90 seconds summed up how much soccer and these boys had meant to him over the years. His voice choked as he said to the parents of underclassmen, "If you get half as much enjoyment out of the game as my wife and I, then you'll be very lucky indeed."

It was the highlight of the night.

David made his college varsity team as a freshman, and Dick had a new team to cheer for. He followed the squad up and down the East Coast. Every player soon knew him, and loved him. A group of parents brought food, and tailgated with the team after each match. Dick was always the center of attention, complimenting the athletes, commiserating with the coach, looking ahead to the next contest.

Of course, he remained loyal to Staples High School. He called me regularly for updates, and arranged his work schedule so he could slip out and see the team play a few times each fall.

He phoned on weekends, too. "Hey Dan, Columbia's at Army tomorrow. Want to go?" No, I'd say; too much work, or we have a game ourselves. "Well, what about LIU at Fordham? That's a little closer. Besides, Fordham plays David's team soon, and I want to get a look at them." Dick loved soccer almost as much as he loved his son. And that was saying something.

I thought of all those things and more as I walked up the driveway to the house. As a coach, I've made these visits more times than I care to count. They're never easy, and I always wonder what to say.

That time, I needn't have worried. Inside the house, I was amazed to see several ex-players gathered around David. Some were already home from college for Easter or Passover when they heard the news; others dropped everything and rushed back to Connecticut to do what they could. One was still en route from Colorado.

Soccer was the glue that helped keep the family together that weekend. Parents comforted Dick's wife; players helped David in their own way. It was a bittersweet team reunion. Just a month remained before most would graduate from college. Final exams and job interviews preyed on their minds, but all knew instinctively that this was the highest priority of all.

The funeral was something to see. More than 500 people packed the temple. Everyone who knew Dick was there, and many had soccer connections. The rabbi was at his eloquent best, but the most memorable lines came when he read from a letter David had written to Dick just a few days before he died.

After calling his father a hero for all he had done, David reminisced about what a great soccer influence Dick had been. David thanked him for his years of support, then mentioned one indelible college memory. It was an away match, played in a monsoon, David wrote, and no one was there – not even for the home team. No one, that is, except his father, leaning against a fence, yelling happily, "Go get 'em, guys!" Appreciative, tear-choked chuckles rippled through the pews.

After the service, the soccer players returned to college. Many wrote fond, remembrance-filled letters to the family; then, slowly, life returned to normal. A month later David graduated. He joined his former teammates as members of the work force, young men who suddenly became adults and were about to go their separate ways. They still saw each other, of course, but their paths were ready to fork. I felt glad that soccer kept them together, and knew it would see them through so much in the future – the bad times as well as the good.

The specifics of this story are unique – one town, one team, one group of players and parents – but the story itself is not. Variations are repeated dozens of times each day, in cities and suburbs all over the United States, wherever youth soccer is played. Several years later, right here in Westport, a funeral and reception for a dad who also tied far too young (and, like Dick, a former player who loved the game yet never interfered) ended a couple of hours later with his sons and their friends heading off to play a pick-up game.

The camaraderie, caring and compassion that imperceptibly grow and envelop a team during its existence is evident everywhere, across the nation. Those feelings remain for years, long after a team ceases to exist. They flower again, whenever there is a wedding, reunion or funeral. The memories of games, trips and seasons shared outlast the specific scores, win-loss records and individual statistics. The latter fade into insignificance, while the former grow in importance with each passing year.

Youth soccer is a valuable experience for everyone involved: players, parents and coaches. Sometimes, though, the most important game is played long after the final goal was scored.

MORE TRAVEL TALES – PART III

"Woog knows all."

For years that was the word on the street (or at least on our trips). From soccer generation to soccer generation, the word was passed down: I knew everything that happened, to everyone, all the time. Sometimes, it was said, I knew things before the rest of the players. Once or twice, legend had it, I knew even before the player/perpetrator himself.

I did nothing to discourage such speculation. The more the boys thought I knew, the less they would try to do. Of course, the counterargument held water too: The more they thought I knew, the greater their incentive to try to outfox me.

It was not particularly hard to learn much of what was going on. All I had to do was remain reasonably alert. The teenage habit of looking past adults as if we don't exist extends to speaking, too. Kids say the darnedest things, many times well within my earshot. Sometimes players get lulled into complacency because they assume that if I'm reading a book or newspaper, I can't hear them. Sometimes I'm not even doing that; I guess they think my bored look means I've tuned them out. When they huddle in a corner, recounting the latest escapade I'm not supposed to know about, their furtive looks draw more attention than neon signs. Even then, their idea of a whisper is many decibels louder than a grown-up's.

Narcs help too, of course. On any trip, one or two boys are so eager to scramble into my good graces that they tell me everything that goes on. I don't encourage such quislings, but I'd be a fool not to listen to their reports. Francis Bacon said "Knowledge is power," and the more knowledge a soccer coach has about his team, the more power he wields on and off the field.

I actually told the players before we left for Europe that I would know 80 percent of what happened immediately, or soon after, it occurred. I'd learn another 10 percent after we get home, and another 5 percent in the ensuing years. Five percent, I said, I'd never know – and that's the way it should be. They did their damnedest to lower the percentages, but they never could. They're teenagers, after all. They are genetically incapable of shutting up – and so are their friends.

But that did not stop them from trying. They tried, for example, the day we arrived in Verona, for the Italy Cup. We settled into the classroom that would serve as our "home" for the next several days. Kids staked out various corners of the room, some as far from the coach as possible, others as close to the window they thought offered prime sneak-out possibilities (unfortunately for them, it did not open far enough). Soon everyone scattered, to check out the rest of the school (how close were the girls teams?) and vicinity (how near were the gelato shops?). My assistant coach and I stayed in the room, doing paperwork.

Not long thereafter – scarcely enough time for anyone to get in trouble, but these guys had it down to a science – a boy slinked into the room, trying to leave with the medical kit without me seeing him. No such luck.

I asked why he needed the kit. "Oh, I don't know. I think somebody cut themselves," he offered lamely. (*Tip to young players: If you are covering up the truth, invent a plausible story before being confronted by your coach.*)

"I'll help," I offered brightly.

"Nothat'sokayit'snothingreally," he said. He might as well have worn an orange highway worker's vest emblazoned with the words "Guilty!"

"So why do you need the med kit?" I countered logically.

"Well…." he said, and the story poured out. His buddy Cameron – who never needed to seek out trouble, because it always found him first

– had met some Italian boys in the courtyard. They had a motorbike. Cameron did his American entrepreneurial thing, trading a T-shirt for a ride. Cameron did not, however, know how to ride a motorbike. On his first turn he slid along the ground, burning his lower leg on the exhaust pipe. His buddy said it looked pretty gruesome. Cameron needed all kinds of ointment and gauze pads. But I wasn't supposed to know, so please, would I not say how I found out?

Knowledge is power, remember, and this little knowledge factoid offered an exceptional opportunity to consolidate my power base. I dispatched my assistant to see whether Cameron needed actual medical treatment, such as stitches or amputation, or if he could simply be slathered and gauzed into recovery. If he needed a doctor, I had to know; if not, I'd be content to sit on the scoop.

Cameron would live, my assistant reported, so I decided to have some fun. For the next couple of days I watched with barely disguised glee as the team went through heroic contortions to keep me from learning about Cameron's mishap. They "snuck" ointment and gauze from the medical kit to keep treating him. I innocently asked why he was wearing long pants when the weather was so hot, then watched him squirm. (*Reminder to young players: If you are covering up the truth, invent a plausible story before being confronted by your coach*). I hovered nearby before a game, as he nervously attempted to don shin guards and socks without showing his battle scars. A few players realized I knew – they could not say anything directly to me, of course -- and found the cat-and-mouse game hilarious.

Finally, after a morning match, I decided to put Cameron out of his psychological misery. (His leg was not looking real good either.) We debated our afternoon plans, with the players lobbying for (what a surprise) free time. I pretended to resist, and finally relented. There was only one condition, I said: "Absolutely no motorbike riding. You never know what can happen. I mean, if someone crashes and burns his leg on the exhaust – I'd have to send him home."

There was a pause, then raucous laughter. "Cameron!" everyone yelled.

He just stared, his eyes wider than dual pipes.

"Woog knows all," I said smugly.

The narcs worked overtime the night Brett mooned the Danish girls.

We were enjoying a home stay in Gudumholm, a tiny town in the Jutland region of Denmark. Actually, it was not tiny; it was infinitesimal. There were a couple of hundred people in the entire town, a place not even the Danish folks I knew in Connecticut had heard of. "I am sure it is a nice place," they said before we left, their dubious stares clearly conveying that my players would be bored stiff.

Gudumholm turned out to be the highlight of our stay. The villagers were astoundingly friendly, the soccer was excellent, and the boys even found a disco to hang out at ("How come Gudumholm has a disco and Westport doesn't?" they asked, quite logically). Best of all, Gudumholm was in the middle of its annual Summer Festival. Food tents ringed the soccer clubhouse; bands played, townspeople put on skits, and kids of all ages enjoyed rides and games. There was even a little parade through town which we, the American visitors, led off as guests of honor.

Our boys leaped easily into the festivities. A Canadian girls team was in Gudumholm at the same time, and their coaches and parents looked stunned that such a small town could maintain such revelry for three days. They imposed a rule that no girl could leave the food tents – okay, they were more like beer tents – unless accompanied by an adult. Both the Gudumholm and Westport boys wrote the Canadians off as a lost cause, and decided to make their own fun.

Which they did, like teenagers all over the world. One international form of mischief seems to be mooning. I don't know how it started in

Gudumholm, but late on our final evening Brett shined a particularly pale moon not far from the festival. Within minutes his spectacularly unloyal teammates had told me about it. Brett was popular, a team leader both at his central midfield position and off the field, but that hardly mattered. The guys knew I'd have fun with the news.

"Get him over here!" I barked, pretending to be mad. But then I softened: "And don't say anything. I'll pretend to take him off to the side and yell at him. You guys can sneak up, but not where I can see you. This should be funny, but try not to laugh."

It did not take long for them to produce Brett. "Dan wants to see you, and man is he pissed!" were the exact words they used.

I motioned Brett over to the side, away from the team. "Get out of here!" I yelled at the others. "This is between Brett and me."

I walked to a quieter area – though I knew the players followed behind – and began to yell. "What the hell is going on?" I asked.

"What do you mean?" Brett feigned innocence.

"You know goddamn well what's going on!" I roared. "The chief of police just came over and talked to me. He said you exposed yourself to someone!"

Brett laughed. "Yeah, I guessed I mooned them," he said. He was sure I'd find the situation as humorous as he.

"Jesus Christ! You *mooned* them! Do you know what you did? Do you have any idea what mooning means in Denmark? Do you know it's just about the worst thing you can do in this culture? Do you know how offensive it is? Well, do you?"

Brett did not know. Neither did I -- or anyone else in Denmark, for that matter. How could they? I made it all up, on the spot. But the inner Dustin Hoffman in me was busting forth. Brett looked worried. I moved in for the kill.

"I spent 15 minutes apologizing for you to the cops, to the parents, to everyone else!" I shrieked. I pretended not to hear the suppressed giggles behind me. Brett had to contend not only with my rage, but with his teammates watching him squirm. "Do you know what they wanted to do? They wanted to *send you home*, that's how bad mooning is considered in this country! I had to talk to them for 15 minutes to convince them not to send you home! Do you think that's how I want to spend tonight? Do you? *Do you?!*"

I had worked myself into a frenzy. By that point, I had almost convinced myself that mooning was the national offense of Denmark, and the police had actually been involved.

"I'm sorry, Dan!" Brett said. "I didn't know it was so bad. Honest, I didn't..." His voice quivered; tears filled his eyes. And then, just moments before he lost it – in front of his teammates, who were both enjoying the show and delighted that they themselves were not in the hot seat – I lost it first. I tried to stop myself, but could not. I cracked up laughing. The boys behind me did the same.

Brett immediately knew he'd been had. His tears vanished. He wanted to be angry, but the only person to be mad at was himself. So he did the only thing he could. He called me a dick, and vowed to get me back.

I readily admitted to his charge, but pointed out I was joined in dickhood by all his teammates. As for getting me back, I told Brett he didn't have a chance. He never would. And he never did.

Although I did spend the rest of the trip looking over my shoulder, waiting for him to try.

Brett could not get me, but on an earlier trip Travis did. And he got me good.

It took a team effort, of course. It was the final night in Verona, and spirits were high. We had an excellent final dinner, complete with fake "awards," hilarious stories and heartfelt thanks. We went back to our classroom, finished packing, and prepared to leave the next morning for home.

Suddenly there was a high-pitched animal chirp, followed by a scared yelp from a human teenager.

"What was that?" I asked.

"I don't know, Dan!" Travis said. "I think I saw something."

"Saw what?" I demanded.

"Some kind of creature!" he said, worriedly.

The instant I said "Don't worry" it came again: the same high-pitched chirp.

"Aaaargh!" Travis yelled, leaping off his mattress onto another boy's. "I did see it! It's moving!"

Chirp! Chirp! Chirp! It came again and again. By now other boys saw it too; those who did not were just as petrified. The Puritan girls who saw witches in Salem acted just like the boys in Verona, although the Connecticut teenagers were much more scared.

I was not frightened – not much, anyway – but I was getting worried. We had an early departure the next day. I wanted everyone to get some sleep, yet now I had to contend with some sort of animal as it chirped and roamed throughout our room.

It chirped again, and panic set in. "Dan, it's *huge!*" Travis said. "Help! You gotta do something!"

"Do something!" the boys echoed. "It's gonna bite us!"

I had no idea what to do – I had not even seen the thing – so I used my best defense: anger. "Dammit!" I said. "You know why this happened? Because someone left the window open! I always told you guys to shut the windows, and now look what's happened! Do you think I said to shut the window just so I could hear myself talk?!" I have always found it strikingly effective, in times of crisis, to solve a problem by throwing it back at those most affected by it.

By this time there was no denying the direness of the situation. The animal was chirping wildly; the boys raced around the room trying to escape, and even my assistant coach had succumbed to panic. "Dan, you better do something!" he advised.

"What!" I hissed

"Go get the guy," he suggested.

"The guy" was an Italian man who earned a few lira sleeping in the hallway. Nominally he was supposed to be in charge of the school, but no one ever saw him do anything, let alone move. However, he probably had access to a broom; he might even know something about Veronese woodland creatures. The thought of waking him up and trying to explain via sign language what was going on was hardly appealing, but it beat staying in a room with 15 terror-stricken teenagers and one rapidly fading assistant coach.

I found Luigi, Pietro or whatever his name might have been. Sure enough, he was sound asleep, and none too pleased at being hauled down the hall. I threw open the door, revealing a team full of boys clutching each other. Other than heavy breathing, not a sound could be heard.

I pointed to the corner. I made hand motions, trying to mimic a small animal I had never actually seen. I made chirping noises, feeling as foolish as the folks who call Click and Clack, the Tappet Brothers, trying to imitate the squeaks, rumbles and grinding sounds their automobiles make (the same ones their mechanics never hear). I even described what was happening in English, speaking loudly so that Alfonso,

149

Gianluca or whatever his name was might understand. No dice.

"I swear, there's something here!" I shouted. "Right?" I pointed at the players.

"GAAAAAAH!" they yelled.

The animal remained quiet.

The Italian guy looked at me like I was *pazzesco*. The American boys looked at me like I was clueless. My assistant coach looked at me like I was a friggin' idiot.

At last it came again: one single *chirp.* The boys leaped in fear – but Trevor laughed. In fact, he laughed at the same time the animal chirped. Then all the boys started laughing. My assistant laughed. Even the Italian dude – Giorgio, Dino, whatever -- laughed too. *Wait a minute!* I thought. *What's so funny? What's going on?*

At times I am a bit slow on the uptake. It took me longer than it should have – long enough for everyone to really start roaring – before I realized they had finally gotten me. Trevor began chirping, and then I knew that all of them -- the boys, my assistant, the Italian guy – everyone was in on it. The master of practical jokes had been practically joked.

It had taken hours of planning, lots of creativity, tons of teamwork and flawless execution, but they had done it. I had to admire them – after all, aren't those exactly the virtues I preach on the soccer field? They had listened to everything I stressed, and learned perfectly.

So I did the only gracious thing I could. I gave them the finger, turned the lights out, and told them all to go to sleep.

But Italy, Denmark and the rest of Europe pale in comparison to places like Australia and New Zealand. I took a team there once, though they are certainly not easy to get to. Fourteen hours into our 25,000-mile odyssey, while sitting bleary-eyed in the Honolulu airport following a long layover in Denver, a player said with a look of consternation, "Dan, do you realize we're going halfway around the world, and *we're not even out of the country yet?*"

Eventually, of course, we reached New Zealand. In my mind's eye I pictured Australia sitting just a few miles away – the Down Under equivalent of Connecticut and Long Island. Turns out Sydney is a solid two-and-a-half hour plane ride from Auckland – which puts it Florida-distance from Connecticut – and from there we faced a two-hour bus ride to Newcastle. The thought of traveling even two minutes more was beyond what I could bear, until our midfielder/mathematician put things in perspective. "Hey, it's $1/204^{th}$ of our entire trip!" he said, referring to our 17 days times 24 hours. I was too exhausted to attempt a comeback.

Yet there is something to be said about arriving somewhere at 8 p.m., nearly 48 hours after setting out. Your hosts realize you're bone-tired, so they feed you some food, hand you an Outback-sized beer, and hustle you off to bed. I woke up 12 hours later completely refreshed, without the slightest hint of jet lag. The boys, dispersed in different homes, all reported feeling just as chipper. I did not ask if they too had been offered continent-sized beers.

Besides our destination, this was a unique trip for me in that we stayed in four separate locations – Newcastle, Sydney, Brisbane and Auckland – and at each site were billeted with host families. Because July is winter Down Under, our hosts were in school. In each city we were trotted into classrooms and presented as show-and-tell objects. That was not particularly objectionable. Our boys loved being treated as celebrities (even if most questions they fielded centered on the incredible amount of racism, drugs and crime the U.S. was perceived to have). At the same time, the host players enjoyed a break from routine.

The lunchtime tradition of "barbies" in the school courtyard got high marks (though no one knew what to make of the girls in Newcastle who, unable to get in, stood outside with pens and scraps of paper, clamoring for autographs of the boys from the States).

But the more schools they saw, the more the Americans became educational experts. They had a hard time understanding why every school in both countries looked the same: small, spartan, austere and cold (all lacked central heating). When I explained this was a function of state control of education, they found it astonishing that a central government could dictate such standards. But they also marveled at the loose, easygoing relationship between staff and students, and soon realized that in education, what goes on inside a classroom is ultimately more important than what that classroom looks like.

Ultimately, however, the Americans were appalled at the low emphasis on academics. They could not believe that all students wore uniforms, though the schools had no legal means of enforcing that rule. They were similarly stunned to learn that Scripture reading is part of the Australian curriculum, and caning is lawful in New Zealand. The boys came away with a tremendous appreciation of their own high school's buildings, facilities, faculty and opportunities (not that they ever conveyed that thanks to their teachers when school began in September).

On a more humorous note, our high schoolers were chagrined to find out they would be playing a first grade team. I pretended not to care – "I'm sure they're pretty good, if they scheduled us" – because I had been warned that "first grade" means the best team in a particular category.

It may have been winter, but both countries' emphasis on sports was astonishing. Classes were dismissed to watch our games; playing in front of 1,000 spectators became routine. We saw more cricket pitches, rugby ovals, racetracks, indoor sports centers and lawn bowling clubs than we could count, and watched enough televised games of all types to fill ESPN airtime for decades. In the Auckland airport, as we waited for our (endless) return flight home, the All Blacks -- New Zealand's legendary national rugby team – strode past. They were surrounded by security guards, and trailed by adoring fans. It was like seeing, in Europe, Barcelona. Two weeks earlier, our soccer players would not have given New Zealand rugby players a second glance. Now they realized the importance of the game to Kiwi culture. And, as athletes, they respected world champions, in any sport.

"Those guys are *huge!*" one boy said to me, in awe. "How can such a small country grow such enormous guys?"

Rugby had figured in another incident a few days earlier. Returning from a match of the Parramatta Eels– how great a name is that? – four of our boys and three host players were mugged on a train. They were upset and mad about losing their wallets, but far angrier about being jumped from behind without a chance to fight back. That, more than anything else, fueled their adolescent senses of injustice and machismo.

Our players found it ironic too that this came just hours after being grilled by Australian students about the high rate of American crime. None of our boys had ever been victimized in the States. "I wish we could back to their school and tell them that," one muttered.

But Australia and New Zealand were, in the end, two of the friendliest countries I have ever seen. Australia meshes its British heritage (left-hand driving, accent, tea) with American openness, equality and spirit of adventure. It makes for an admirable combination. (Just don't ask where Vegemite, the yeast, salt and riboflavin paste smeared on every food imaginable -- which looks like mildewed motor oil but does not taste nearly as good -- comes in).

Australia was also the first nation I visited where Americans were admired, even revered. Time after time, hearing our accents, elderly Australian strangers came up to thank us for our country's contributions during World War II. Our players had no concept of what we had done –

nor, to be brutally honest, did I, until I asked – but the boys had the grace and intelligence to say thanks.

Then again, when it came to history, our players were Will and Ariel Durant compared to their Australian peers. We were there during that nation's bicentennial, but we found most Australians had little sense of the past. "The convicts came, and now we're here" was one boy's summation of his nation's heritage.

Such honesty was never far from the surface. Australians love the United States, but they know we are not without problems. "We follow you Yanks' lead in everything," we heard time and again. "We just hope we can learn from your mistakes."

Speaking of lessons, the boys learned a very important one midway through the trip: Be careful what you wish for, because it might come true. They had already stayed with two sets of host teams, and flew to Brisbane eager for the third. They had long ago shaken off their unease at meeting new families, and staying in unfamiliar homes. By that point in the trip they were vying with each other to see who would have the four most diverse living arrangements.

We stepped off the plane and into the terminal, searching for our hosts. Oddly enough, there were no soccer-type guys to be seen. There was, however, an entire group of healthy, busty teenage girls, looking eagerly around.

"Too bad we're not staying with *them*," one of our players said. The rest just leered, or drooled.

At that moment the bustiest girl stepped forward.

"Are you West-poat?" she asked, in a charming accent.

"Yes," I said, momentarily confused. Had our hosts sent their girlfriends to greet us?

"Welcome to Brisbane!" she said. "We're your 'osts!"

In all my years of coaching, I had never seen an entire team speechless. No, they were beyond that; they were dumbstruck, thunderstruck, every kind of struck. Their eyes grew as wide as soccer goals, but try as they might they could not speak.

"Well, come along!" the self-appointed leader said. "We 'aven't got all day!"

The boys looked at each other as if each had won the lottery and World Cup simultaneously. They picked up their bags, followed the girls and – with a minimum of rib-poking and mental undressing – began their four-day stay in the appropriately named state of Queensland.

Each morning when the team gathered, they shared stories of the previous night: the parties and discos they attended, the other girls their 'osts introduced them to, the awesome time they were having. Our ostensible reason for being in Brisbane – for the entire trip, actually – was to demonstrate soccer skills at the U.S. Pavilion at that city's International Expo, but soccer seemed to take a back seat to hanging out with our shapely host team.

When the Brisbane leg of the trip came to an end we gathered at the airport to fly back to Sydney, then on to New Zealand. The two teams hugged goodbye, and once again we were on our own: a bunch of American guys, alone together halfway around the world.

"So how was it?" I asked. I expected a chorus of cheers and growls, a high-five or two, perhaps a suggestion that from now on, every team I took overseas should be 'osted by girls.

Instead I heard silence. No one said anything for a long, long time.

Finally, one boy broke the ice.

"You know, Dan," he said, "it really wasn't that great. I don't know why, but it wasn't what I thought it would be."

"I don't know about you guys, but I always had to be on my best behavior," someone said.

"It was like I always had to impress them," a teammate added.

"Yeah, I always felt like I was showing off for them," noted a fourth.

A cascade of complaints rained down: They could never relax in the house, because they were with girls, not guys. The girls were not like guy players, yet because they were also not brother/sister or boyfriend/girlfriend, no one could ever figure out their relationships.

Then one boy delivered the final verdict: "She was always around, so for four days I couldn't fart." His teammates nodded in full agreement, complete understanding and total relief.

Several hours later, as the plane taxied to the terminal in Auckland, I turned to the team. "So, what do you want: girls or guys?"

"Guys!" they announced, unanimously.

"WE DIDN'T 'LAWST...'"

Planning a youth soccer trip takes time. There are application, permission-to-travel and roster forms to fill out, copy and mail in. There is housing to book, transportation to arrange, information to relay to players and parents, last-second changes to cope with. D-Day took more organization, but not much.

Which is why a spur-of-the-moment, completely unorganized two-day summer jaunt to Long Island was perhaps the greatest tournament of my youth soccer life.

Like abiogenesis or spontaneous combustion, this trip blossomed out of nowhere. One afternoon I was sitting at the beach, talking with a couple of former players who had just graduated from high school; the next morning I, several of their buddies and a few more they had never played formally with but knew by reputation were packed into three or four cars headed through rush-hour traffic to an event we knew little about. All we heard, in fact, was that somebody had a college buddy who had a friend of a friend of a friend who said one of the registered teams had backed out, and hoped we could come down to salvage the bracket.

So we did. We were a ragtag bunch spanning five or so years, from high school through college. The players did all the organizing, which meant making a few phone calls to see who was available, agreeing what color T-shirts to wear, tossing food, beverages and ice into coolers, wrangling cars from their parents, and somehow finding a map of Long Island. I was invited along as the "coach," though the guys promised they would handle most of the substituting and related issues themselves. Substitutions turned out to be irrelevant; they mustered only 11 players.

For a control freak like me -- a man who usually takes charge of every detail -- it was a welcome change. Here was a chance to see whether all my theories about soccer being a Petri dish for maturity and responsibility were true, or bullshit. It was also an opportunity to enjoy a couple of days out of town, in the relaxed company of a group of players I truly liked, who themselves loved soccer yet had never been together as a team. I felt like an anthropologist about to study a newly discovered tribe.

The tournament organizers seemed as loosey-goosey as us. Registration procedures usually involve the presentation of signed, sealed and notarized documents; scrutiny of player identification far beyond what even a gun-toting Afghan undergoes at U.S. airports, and the dissemination of enough rule books, programs and errata to stock a library.

This time we breezed in, said, "Yo, we're here – Westport," and received a hand-written schedule. Directions to the field were drawn in pencil.

We played three games that day, and won them all. Our players had two things going for them. One was that, having all come through the Westport system, they played the same style of soccer, so it hardly mattered that the opening match was the first time they had worked together. The second advantage was that they had the time of their lives. With absolutely no pressure, they relaxed and enjoyed themselves. It was soccer the way it ought to be. Damn good soccer, too.

There were a couple of bumps along the way, of course. One boy had to go back to Connecticut; he was due in court in the morning, on an underage-possession-of-alcohol charge. A second one suffered a huge gash above his eye. We of course had no medical kit, and this was not the type of tournament with doctors and nurses prowling the sidelines. So I sent him to the hospital with one of our players, and prayed they would find their way back to us. In those pre-cellphone days, that was by no means a sure bet.

We felt pretty good that evening, having won three games (scoring, I might add, a couple of world-class goals in the process) to launch ourselves, somehow, into the semifinals. That's when we realized it had gotten late. It would be ridiculously unproductive to drive two hours back home, then two more returning at the crack of dawn. No one had thought ahead to the possibility we would still be playing the next day, so we improvised. We decided to find a motel.

That was the hardest part of the trip. Every place was filled, either by soccer teams or families vacationing at nearby beaches. Just as we were about to give up and sleep in our cars – talk about your bonding experience! – we spotted a place that looked like it had been scouted as the Bates Motel in "Psycho," but rejected as too scary-looking.

Excitedly, we checked in. The guys spread out their T-shirts and shorts to dry (which, happily, made the rooms smell better). A few remembered to call their parents to say they would not be home. Soon we all headed off in search of a place fit for a celebratory, but very cheap, dinner.

Fortunately, Long Island is the diner capital of the western world. We feasted, then headed back to the only motel in the western world without televisions. That fazed our boys not at all; they were having too much fun wrestling and airing out their rooms.

The next morning, heading into the semifinals, our low numbers caught up with us. With our underage drinker gone (he eventually beat the rap; obviously, he argued, the beer in the trunk of his car belonged to his father) we were down to 10 players. The young man who probably had a concussion gave it his best shot, despite being unable to head. That poses a major problem for a defender, which is what he was, so we wrapped his skull in a huge turban, moved him up front, told him to run around as a decoy and hoped he would not injure himself further. Five minutes in he bulled his way through the goalmouth, got knocked to the ground, and bled like a stuck pig the rest of the match.

The boys, meanwhile, had whipped themselves into a frenzy. They had created instant traditions – chants, celebrations, even a ritualistic group urination (don't ask) – and rode the power of those emotions as far as they could. But our foes – an Austrian team, hosted by the Long Island club sponsoring the tournament – were excellent. The match remained deadlocked.

Suddenly, with just a few minutes remaining, the referee called a penalty kick against us. I learned long ago that complaining about officials' calls is useless. They all even out over time, and a team that doesn't score has more things to worry about than one call against them. However, I can state with complete honesty that this particular penalty kick was bullshit. The referee, who no doubt was a host father for the Austrian kid who took a dive in the box, had it in for the happy-go-lucky boys from just across Long Island Sound. Obviously he hated Westport's chants, celebrations and ritualistic group urination.

The game ended with a heartbreaking one-goal loss. Suddenly, the emotion of the previous 48 hours washed over our players – the same ones who, two days earlier, had been lounging in Connecticut without a clue they'd soon play four intense matches with players they'd never taken the field with before. Two or three of them cried, something they had not done even after losing high school championships. One pleaded with me to appeal the game. No, I said gently. Even if we'd had an airtight reason, this was not the type of tournament that planned ahead for an appeals board.

I was stunned by the depth of the players' feelings. Clearly the two days had reached deep into their soccer-playing souls, and for that I was grateful. But when the boys started yapping about the injustice of it all, how'd they'd come all that way (granted, not as far as the Austrians) only to be robbed by a stupid friggin' ref who favored Austrians over Americans, the reaction seemed to be getting out of hand.

Just as suddenly, reality intruded. One of the spectators – a girl who had cheered for the Austrian boys her family had hosted – walked up to the most agitated of our many overwrought players. In a hideous Long Island accent that could have come straight out of a "Saturday Night Live" parody of "Saturday Night Fever," she said, "Yaw just mad dat yoo lawst."

The very upset boy stared at her. His eyes brimmed with tears, but he said, calmly, clearly, and in tones usually reserved for particularly dim children: "No. I'm sorry. We didn't 'lawst.' We 'lost.'"

At which his nine teammates – now as tight as if they'd spent their entire soccer-playing careers together – guffawed, punched and high-fived him for his witty comeback.

In an instant, all was right with the world. We got in our cars, headed for home, passed by Shea Stadium, said what the hell and stopped off to watch the Mets.

They lawst too.

JOE

Joe was not the sharpest knife in the drawer. A wonderful kid –
outgoing, enthusiastic, do anything for you, as skilled with his hands as
he was athletic with his feet – but when God passed out common sense,
Joe was off in the corner juggling.

Logic was not Joe's strong suit. Early one spring, he missed practice.
I seldom follow up on isolated absences, but this was one of those
occasions where a player's buddies can't wait to rat him out. They were
13, and with a mixture of pride, envy, hormones and back-stabbing, they
immediately piped up. "You know why Joe's not here, don't you? His
mom's away, and he's with his *girlfriend.*" Joe and Alice had been dating
for at least a day, so by seventh grade standards they were practically
common-law.

As soon as practice ended, I called Joe's house. No answer. I tried
several more times; still no Joe. I wondered whether they had done
something really stupid, like eloped, then realized Joe would have had
no idea what the word meant even if Alice wanted to.

Finally, at 8 p.m., Joe picked up the phone. "We missed you today,"
I said.

"I know," he replied, oozing regret. "I was" – here he paused,
searching for just the right excuse – "sick."

"That's too bad," I said. "But Joe, I tried to call earlier. If you were
sick, why didn't you answer?

Now, you, I or most average Joes would have had a quick
comeback: "I was asleep." "I was at the doctor's." "I was puking my
brains out."

Joe's head never worked that way. "Oh!" he perked up, as if he just
remembered. "I was out raking leaves!"

"Um, Joe," I said. "It's March."

"I know," Joe countered, using the same "who-me?" innocence Bill Clinton trotted out a bit later. "My mom was bugging me to rake the yard since last fall. So when I got sick I figured, why not go outside now and do it?"

Joe got off scot-free, of course. A line like that was too good for punishment. Besides, in a perverse way, I wanted to teach his teammates a lesson: You don't narc on someone just because he's doing something you'd do yourself if you ever got the chance. It doesn't take Alfred Einstein, as Joe once called him, to know that most seventh graders would choose "raking leaves" over school any day of the week.

A couple of years later I saw another side of Joe's unique mind. We were overseas; we'd spent the first few wonderful days playing soccer in and around Konstanz, Germany (and, much to our host team's surprise, winning). Now they took us to the Austrian Alps.

It was an incredible excursion. We hiked long and hard (and more than one player suspected we were being intentionally tired out for the game that night – *ach*, those Germans think of everything). But the spectacular views were worth it: snow-capped peaks, storybook villages, straight-out-of-central-casting mountain goats and yodelers. If the kids had any idea what "Heidi" was, they would have compared it to that.

At midday we arrived at a wooden lodge for a "grill-fest." We hungrily devoured sausages, bratwurst, schnitzel, potatoes – your basic pre-game meal – and each player got one Coke. Being 15, however, a mere 8,000 calories was not enough, so the boys bought more: ice cream, candy, and of course Cokes. They paid for the extras with the money they had: German marks. Because we were in Austria, they received change in schillings.

Joe turned to me, his eyes wide. "Dan, look!" he said. "I'm rich!"

"What do you mean?" I asked.

"I gave them like 20 markses, and got all this back." He was right: His hand held about 800 schillings.

I should not have tried to explain international economics to Joe, but the high mountain air must have gotten to me. "No," I said. "It's the same *amount* of money. It's just a different type of currency is all. Germans use marks, Austrians use schillings, we use dollars. It's different names, but it's all the same money."

Joe peered at me as if I should be pitied, a grossly retarded person unable to understand such basic concepts as "less" and "more." "Dan," he repeated, "I'm rich. Look at all this money!"

His friends were no help; they were laughing too hard. I was alone on this one.

"Joe," I said, using rationality when only a 2-by-4 would have worked. "What do you think will happen when you change back to marks?"

Joe was way ahead of me. He'd already thought this through, and boy, was I the village idiot. *"I'm not going to!"* he said with infinite patience. *"I'll just keep these things until we get home."*

I don't know if by "home" he meant Konstanz or Westport. But I do know that the next day, Joe was not a happy camper.

"They ripped me off, Dan," he said. "The fucking Germans ripped me off. They took all my things" – I assumed he meant schillings – "and gave me like shit for them."

Descending to ground level had finally cleared my head. "I know, Joe," I said. "Can you believe it? They're bastards."

DADDIES AND MOMMIES

Soccer builds character, we youth coaches are fond of saying. It teaches lifelong lessons like teamwork and loyalty. We're all in this together, we tell parents; we support what you're doing at home, and appreciate your help supporting us. It takes a village to raise a child, as that famous soccer mom Hillary Rodham Clinton once noted. And -- especially for teenagers -- the soccer field may be as important a part of that village as the home, school or mall.

Most parents get it. They may not agree with everything a coach says or does, but they have the common sense and courtesy to hold their tongues when they disagree. Most parents, even today, know they could not do a better job (nor would they care to try). And they recognize that the coach provides several services – fun, skills education, babysitting, therapy, tutoring that will pay off in a college scholarship (!) – at a price far below market cost.

But on every team, one or two sets of parents do not get it. I don't mean occasional bitch-and-moan sessions held in the SUV on the way home from games ("Austin, I cannot believe the coach took you out after scoring four goals. He'll see how valuable you are when we find another team!"). Nor do I refer to the parents who criticize every decision, from tactics, formations and positions ("How dare you play my son at left back? That's the right field of soccer!") to arrival times for matches ("That's ridiculous – it's way too early/late/hard for me to get there after my golf game!").

No; the parents I mean are the ones who say and do things so bizarre, so outlandish, so inconceivable that they must live in a parallel but spectacularly skewed universe. Their methods may be subtle or ham-fisted; their actions vary from year to year, and team to team. But those parents are always there, digging doggedly to undermine the foundation a coach spent years laboriously laying.

These men and women have only one thing in common: Without them, coaches would have far fewer war stories.

Where would I be without Erno, for example? He was an Eastern European immigrant who stunned his son Sev and Sev's teammates by making them stand outside the house during a severe thunder and lightning storm. (They lived closest to the field, but Erno didn't want their wet, sweaty bodies inside.) That should have told me Erno wasn't walking with the rest of the ducks, yet I was still unprepared for the day Sev beat up Patrick.

It happened at school, not soccer practice, but the news traveled quickly. We trained that afternoon and the 12-year-olds raced onto the field, eager to give the blow-by-blow. Neither Sev nor Patrick appeared that day.

Patrick was an excellent defender, as tough as they come on the field but a happy-go-lucky jokester off it; he would much rather look for girls than a fight. Sev was a decent player (though not nearly as good as he or his father thought), and wired pretty tightly. You would be too, I suppose, if your father once buried your television set in the front yard because he didn't like the programming it carried. Naturally, I thought the fight was Sev's fault.

After practice I called Patrick. He was still out of it – the fight had been rough, and I suspected a concussion – and none too forthcoming about the details. All he said was that Sev had come at him without warning, and the fight had something to do with something Patrick said about Sev's sister.

My next call was to Sev. Despite his dysfunctional background, he was raised to be polite to adults. "Oh, hello, Dan," he said. "How are you tonight?"

After an odd exchange of pleasantries, I brought up the fight. "Oh, yes, we fought today," he said. And without my asking, he admitted, "I started it. Patrick said something bad about my sister."

I launched into my teammates-must-not-fight speech. I discussed the importance of unity on the field, and equanimity off it. Everyone didn't have to like everyone else, I said, but we could not have people battling each other. Words were one thing, fisticuffs another. I told Sev I would have to suspend him for one game.

There was silence on his end. He had not expected such harsh punishment.

"But Dan," he said, his 12-year-old bravado giving way to tears. "I had to do it. My father told me if I did not fight for my sister's honor, I could not come home again. And he was very mad. I could tell he meant it."

That posed a quandary. If I punished Sev for fighting, I risked causing trouble at home. If I did not punish him, I risked sending the team a message that fighting was fine. I asked to speak to his father.

I was in my mid-20s, brimming with youthful self-confidence. As a successful coach, I believed I could win anyone over to my side.

"Oh, yes, I sent Sev out to fight today," his father said. "He had to. It was a matter of his sister's honor. I am sure you understand."

"Well, no," I said. "Not exactly. Besides, don't you realize that no matter how you feel personally, Sev is part of the team, and he has to follow team rules. It puts me in a difficult position…."

"Fine," he interrupted. "If that is how you feel, I will remove Sev from the team."

That was the exact opposite of what I wanted, which was to remove Erno from earth. Allowing him to take his son away would alienate Sev from his friends (and 12-year-olds can still be friends, even after fighting each other). It would take him away from soccer, which

Sev loved. And it would prevent me from countering, in whatever small way I could, the influence of a man whose belief in justice was mired back in medieval Transylvania.

So I made a decision. Sev would stay on the team, and would not be punished. I told the team that Sev, his father and I had talked, and such a situation would not happen again. (Though I knew full well that, with Erno's trigger temper, it could reoccur before I finished speaking).

And I made one more decision, one based on my own need for self-preservation: I never spoke another word to Erno.

Off-the-wall behavior is not limited to men, of course. Take Karen, in action one hot afternoon. It was a spring league game, hardly the most important contest on earth, and Karen was one of the few parents who even bothered to come. By the time their kids are U-19, even the most avid mothers and fathers let go. Most, if pressed, would admit to relief that their children can finally drive themselves to matches, pack their own soccer bags, and handle wins and losses without parental help.

But Karen had two sons on the team – Dermott, 19, and Sean, 16 – and she truly loved soccer. So if she wanted to spend a broiling June day watching a humdrum match, instead of lounging at the beach or inside where even I would rather have been, who was I to stop her?

It was so hot, in fact, that Karen held an umbrella over her head. The heat also contributed to flared tempers on the field. That was unusual in a spring game, but then both Dermott and Sean were nudgy, obstreperous players whose pesky perseverance often brought out the worst in opponents.

The referee wisely issued a few yellow cards, perhaps a red or two. When things looked like they were getting further out of hand, I decided to take Sean off the field to cool off. Before I could make that move, though, he got involved in a shoving match with a boy on the other team.

A couple of players on both teams moved to break it up; a few others, emboldened by the heat and their own testosterone, piled on the original combatants. The referee and linesmen moved in to impose order, but before they could act a spectator raced down the hill and onto the field. It might have been a scene straight out of the English or Colombian league – except this fan was female. It was Karen, brandishing her umbrella like a sword.

She tore toward the melee, and before anyone could stop her she pounded her umbrella on...her son Dermott.

"You didn't protect your brother! You didn't help him! You didn't fight for him!" she shrieked. Each sentence was emphasized with a whomp upside Dermott's head. She was a crazed woman, but no one on the field – not the other players, all of whom had stopped fighting; not the referees, who had gathered around in amazement, nor any of the coaches or spectators – could do anything.

We should have tried, of course. We should have pulled her away from her son, calmed her down, helped bring order out of chaos. We should have made sure everyone was all right. At the very least, we should have made sure her umbrella was not broken.

But none of us could do any of that. It was impossible, because we were laughing too hard.

After the game the coach of the other team approached me. He asked if he could hire "that woman with the umbrella" for all his games, in case any more fights broke out.

No way, I said. She's my secret weapon. We all laughed again, before checking nervously to make sure she was nowhere in sight.

OL' MAN RIVER

The nondescript hotel in East Hartford, Connecticut was not where I would normally take a soccer team. For one thing, it was only an hour from Westport. For another, it was the type of place whose lobby bar filled up every Friday evening with secretaries from Hartford insurance companies looking to hook up with executives from other insurance companies – hardly a healthy environment for players competing in a soccer tournament. But our games in the Hartford area ran late that Friday, and we had to be back on the field at the crack of dawn Saturday, so the players and I snagged a few hotel rooms for the night.

We got dinner, the boys played video games, and then I asked them to head upstairs. I knew it would take a while for them to sleep – something about a hotel makes even the most mild-mannered teenager act up – but I figured watching TV and sending messages by tapping on walls was not the worst way they could spend the evening.

My assistant coach and I headed down to the lounge. I am not a big drinker, so I sipped one beer and surveyed the scene. The secretaries, most of them sporting big hair and too much makeup, were putting moves on the businessmen, most of them sporting little hair and dull clothes. Everyone was smoking. A three-man band tinkled in the background. It was depressing as hell, and I was ready to leave.

Out of the corner of my eye I spotted Aaron -- my goalkeeper. He was big for his age, strong, already a daily shaver. He fancied himself quite the ladies' man. In fact, at that very moment he was chatting up a secretary with particularly large hair. But there was another fact: Aaron was only 15 years old.

I nudged my assistant. He was more surprised than I – I'd spent enough time with teenagers to know that if you give them an inch, they'll try to take I-95 all the way from Maine to Florida – and made a move to get up.

I motioned for him to sit. "Let me handle this," I said.

I walked over to Aaron.

"How ya doin'?" I asked casually.

"Oh – hi!" he said. He turned, momentarily flustered, to his new friend. "This is my..." – he searched for the right word. "Coach" obviously would not do; even a box turtle could have figured out that Aaron had not told his new squeeze that he was playing in a soccer tournament with his U-15 team. I had a couple of decades on Aaron; how could he explain our relationship?

"...friend from work," he concluded. "Dan, meet Amber. Amber, Dan." Well, I thought, at least his mother raised him to handle introductions well.

I decided to play along. A happy goalkeeper, after all, is a good goalkeeper. "Nice to meet you, Amber," I said. "And you" – I pointed to Aaron, but did not say his name. Who knew how he had introduced himself? "You, keep up the great work."

I walked back to my table. My assistant, who watched the whole encounter, reported that Aaron gave a quick thumb's up.

We kept an eye on Aaron, just so he would not step too far out of line. Ten or 15 minutes later, however, he stepped somewhere else – right up to the bandleader. The trio had just finished a lounge classic – perhaps "Strangers in the Night" -- and was taking a much-appreciated breather. Aaron and the bandleader conferred. The older man shook his head "no" several times. Aaron kept talking. Finally the bandleader relented.

He took the microphone. "Ladies and gentlemen," he said, "we have a special treat. "Brandon" – so that was his *nom du jour!* – "is a young man studying voice in New York. He'd like to sing a solo. What do you think?"

There was a scattering of applause. Most of the patrons were too bored, drunk or horny to care.

"So let's hear it for Brandon!" the bandleader intoned.

Aaron – er, Brandon – took the mike from him seamlessly, just the way Ike handed off to Tina before their falling out. I knew Aaron – damn it, Brandon – had a good voice; just a couple of months earlier he'd starred in the junior high production of "Showboat." I did not think he would embarrass himself – not completely, anyway, the way I would if I attempted to sing. I just hoped he'd belt out a good, rockin' number that would get all those insurance people off their fat butts and onto the dance floor.

Aaron – I keep forgetting; *Brandon* -- paused for dramatic effect. He looked to the ceiling for inspiration. He opened his mouth.

"Ol' man river, dat ol' man river, he must know sumpin', but don't say nothin', he jes' keeps rollin', he keeps on rollin' along...."

Christ on a bicycle! There we were, at a bar filled with people trying to pick each other up, drunk as skunks to boot, and my goalkeeper was singing the saddest, most mournful song ever heard on a Broadway stage. It was "Ol' Man River" from "Showboat" – the only song, I suddenly realized, that Aaron/Brandon knew.

For several long minutes, he sang. He sang of sweatin' and strainin', of bodies racked with pain; of bein' tired of living, and skeered of dyin', while ol' man river, dat ol' man river, he jes keeps rollin' along. It is a beautiful ballad – interminable, but beautiful – and fits perfectly in the context of the show about life on de Mississippi. It is a classic song in American musical theater, and rightfully so.

But the only poorer selection for a cheesy hotel bar on a Friday night would have been "Taps."

Aaron, aka Brandon's, rendition did not bring down the house. It simply brought everyone down. Insurance executives lifted their hands off secretaries' knees. Secretaries stopped blowing smoke rings in insurance executives' faces. Drinkers stopped drinking, bartenders stopped pouring. The mournful song went on. And on. And on. For many excruciating minutes, my goalkeeper sucked all the energy – physical, sexual and every other kind – out of the hotel lounge.

When it was over, the patrons reacted with relief. They applauded politely, in the manner of the Ed Sullivan act in which a sequined Bulgarian entertainer spun plates atop shaky poles. Then, filled with the overpowering sadness the young singer had introduced into their lives, they filed out of the bar. It was the ultimate buzzkill.

Aaron was oblivious to it all. He took his bow, passed triumphantly by my assistant and me, and returned to his chair next to Amber.

She gazed into his eyes. She took his hand, and clasped it in hers. She smiled adoringly, as if Barry Manilow himself had just stepped into the East Hartford hotel and brought a miracle into her life, and those of all her friends toiling in the insurance industry.

Amber was even dumber than I thought.

A FEW GOOD REASONS TO
LOVE AND HATE YOUTH SOCCER

The scene was Binghamton, New York; the event, the U.S. Youth Soccer Association Eastern Regional tournament. This was as big a deal as it sounds, and our team – which qualified as the Connecticut state champion – was playing strongly. The boys were eager to win it all. But they were also 14 years old, so the connection between getting a good night's sleep and performing well the next day was not exactly clear.

It was after midnight. From my room down the hotel hall I heard laughter. Then I heard yelling. Then banging on walls.

I yanked myself out of bed, and charged down the corridor. I rapped on the door. From behind, I heard the scamper of adolescent feet. Boys jumped into bed – more than the four who were assigned to the room, I was sure. I pounded some more.

"Who is it?" a faux-sleepy voice asked.

"Me!" I yelled. "Open up!"

"Just a minute!" A minute passed; I had no idea what or who was being stashed where. Finally, the door opened.

"What's the matter?" a player asked unctuously.

"What the hell is going on here?!" I thundered.

Innocence prevailed – for five seconds. Suddenly the phone rang. I picked it up. A teenage girl's voice asked for one of the boys – the one who had claimed complete ignorance.

I reacted like an outraged father. "Listen to me, young lady," I snarled. "These are my players, and I want them to go to bed. Don't you dare call any of them again. Do you understand?!" Before she could answer, I slammed down the phone.

I turned to the boys, who watched my performance with various degrees of terror, incredulity, awe and amazement. I was sure that others, hiding in the closet or bathroom, were listening too, too petrified to make a sound.

"You guys have *exactly eight seconds to grow up!* And if you don't, you will *not* play tomorrow – or ever again!" I roared.

One player started to cry.

I turned, wheeled around, yanked the door behind me and clomped back to my room.

I heard not a peep for the rest of the night. As the years passed the boys – now grown men – have delighted in telling that story over and over . It symbolizes adolescent hi-jinks, adult unreasonableness, and the sheer sense of freedom that 14-year-old boys enjoy when they're by themselves in a hotel room with their best friends, their soccer teammates.

Today when they tell that tale, all eyes gravitate toward the boy who took my "eight seconds to grow up" speech literally, and started to cry. Nowadays, he is able to laugh about it.

Well, not exactly laugh. He actually just chuckles along with the rest of his buddies. Sort of.

Two more Binghamton stories, both about sex. Fortunately, neither involves 14-year-olds – at least not directly.

The first began with me making hotel arrangements for the parents and family members who planned to accompany us to that same Eastern Regional tournament. It was a simple request, really: How many rooms do you want, and single or double beds?

But this was Westport – the setting for "The Stepford Wives." I knew that Terry's mother and "stepfather," Anne and Bob, presented themselves as a couple, but were not technically married. I also knew that Terry's dad, Angus, was on friendly terms with Anne and Bob. But I had no idea how close they were until Anne mentioned that all three of them would travel to Binghamton.

"So two rooms?" I asked, reasonably enough.

"Oh, no," she replied. "All we need is one."

Yikes! "Well, you know, they're not real expensive," I said. "And there are still plenty of rooms available."

"No problem," she said, tossing her hot potato right back at me. "We'll do fine. Besides, we take all our vacations together."

TMI. And I certainly did not want the players to have any of the "I" about this arrangement. I myself didn't mind, mind you – far be it for me to care what adults do in the privacy of their hotel rooms – but I was concerned that the boys would pepper Terry with too many questions.

So added to my task that long weekend was one more: making sure my players were off the floor whenever Anne, Bob and Angus might happen to come in or out. So to speak.

The second Binghamton sex story took place two years later. Once again we were state champions, representing Connecticut at the Eastern Regionals. This time, however, the boys were U-16. A team from another town had won the U-19 age group. Hotels were allocated by state, though if the idea was to foster closeness and pride, it bombed. Our two towns were bitter rivals, and though the age groups were different, our team and theirs did not really care for the other. Okay, they hated each other.

What our players and theirs did share were housing arrangements: four boys to a room, two in each double bed. It was tight, but it was cheap. Everyone adapted easily – until our players caught on that the U-19 team's star player was not sharing his bed, or even his room, with a teammate. He was hardly unpopular or lonely; his girlfriend was right there to perk him up.

I should probably mention here that this young man's father was the coach of the team.

"Dan, how come we can't share a room with our girlfriends?" my players asked.

"First of all, because your parents would kill me," I said. "Second of all, because everyone else in Westport would kill me too. Third of all, most of you guys don't even have girlfriends. And fourth of all, my room is right next to his" – meaning the 19-year-old stud muffin. "Those two keep me up all night. So if you had your 'girlfriends' up, you'd never get any sleep. And you wouldn't want that, would you?"

"We could handle it," one boy suggested.

"Dan, if we win the U-19 state cup in three years, will you let us bring girls?" another asked.

"Yeah," I said. They looked at me in stunned amazement, and utter respect.

"Just as soon as you can walk to the planet Zork," I added.

The Bartlett twins came to Westport in ninth grade. That is a difficult age to move to a suburban town, and try to break into the social scene. Soccer usually helps, but because the Bartletts were shy – and had each other as friends – they seldom hung out with the guys. Their teammates, meanwhile, were perfectly content to continue their long-established friendships, and not extend themselves to the new twin faces in town.

From my adult perspective, I thought that was ridiculous. The Bartletts were nice, intelligent, good-looking, and very good players – just like most of their teammates. But I also knew it is impossible to force teenagers to be friends with anyone they do not want to be. I suspected that, as they grew older, the Bartletts' social lives would improve, and they would be welcomed into the team's inner circle.

It happened, though more slowly than I expected. By that time everyone was ready for college, heading off in separate directions. The Bartletts went to the same school, and slipped from their teammates' radar.

Several years later they reappeared. In college they had grown bigger, stronger, more self-confident – and even better looking. On vacation in Miami they met the owner of a modeling agency. He liked what he saw, sent them for head shots, liked those even more, and offered to represent them. They chucked their 9-to-5 jobs, and became male models.

Actually, they became supermodels. They worked with Cindy Crawford, and were photographed by Herb Ritts. They divided their time between Los Angeles, South Beach and Milan. For the first time, their former teammates were interested in the Bartlett twins.

The Bartletts, meanwhile, had the last laugh. They were red-hot. Women flocked to them. And they made $60,000 per shoot.

Each.

As a youth soccer coach, I have learned to rejoice in the happy endings like the Bartletts'. It is a delight to watch boys grow into men. Frequently, the men they become are happy, healthy and successful, in whatever ways one measures such things. They find their passion, be it finance, law, medicine, art, technology, cooking or anything else. They find a partner, make a home, become part of any type of community that is important to them. They keep in touch (some more than others, for sure). They continue to play soccer, coach their own children or others, or simply tune in to the World Cup every four years. They move on with their lives, at the same time keeping a small part of their soccer adolescence close at hand.

Happily, that happens to most of the young men I coach. Unhappily, it does not happen to all.

Some of the best – the strongest, swiftest, most dedicated, most intelligent, most creative; the ones with the most going for them -- have crashed and burned.

Alcohol and drugs take some of them down. Emotional problems like schizophrenia and depression can lurk for years inside their bodies before striking. Some, supremely confident on the youth soccer field, lose that swagger in college, on the trading floor, or in the bedroom. They suddenly find themselves different people than they ever were before, and they cannot cope. Some are unlucky in business or love. That happens to nearly everyone of course, at one time or other, but for some reason these particular people cannot rise above a temporary setback.

It is easy to predict which youngsters will be unsuccessful in life – easy, and not always accurate. I have been wrong on more than one occasion. A boy I wrote off as a hopeless goofball turns out years later to have an uncanny knack for cracking the books, making money, or finding a lover who turns his life around. Those mistakes I am delighted to make.

But I have also been wrong in predicting a limitless future for too many young people whose horizons turn out to have sharp limits. Too often I have answered the phone at 3 a.m., because a former player pleads to be bailed out of jail yet again. Too often I have heard former players describe a teammate's descent into an unimaginable personal hell. Too often I have passed a sad-looking, homeless-type person on the street; he has called my name, and I realize it is a former star.

Each time that happens, I grow angry. Perhaps, I tell myself, I could have done something differently during the time we shared on the soccer field. Perhaps I could have extended myself more off the field. Perhaps I missed the warning signs that should have been so obvious. But then I think about the many success stories I have been blessed to know, and realize they had little to do with me. Their parents' influence on those players, their friends, genes, environment and luck, had far more to do with their accomplishments than anything I said or did during the few seasons we spent together. I am glad for their achievements, but I do not congratulate myself for them. So why should I beat myself up over those few who have failed?

I know all that is true. Yet each time it happens I go back to my current team, and vow that our next session together will be the best we ever had.

Westport does not exactly teem with minorities. It's a typical Fairfield County suburb: upscale and white. But every year or two I had a black player on my team. For several years, that number doubled: we had two.

They were different, Adam and Pierre. Adam was a big, fast, well-skilled and versatile player; his father, a business executive, was quite wealthy. Pierre was not as quick, had average skills, and had to fight to keep his starting spot. Both of Pierre's parents worked, and the family struggled to live in Westport. Both Adam and Pierre were long-time team members, but not particularly close friends. Each had his own group he felt most comfortable with. That was natural; the color of their skin did not necessarily bind them together.

One weekend when they were 14, we headed to Long Island for the Hicksville Indoor Tournament. This was an annual winter highlight: a slam-bang affair featuring great teams, tons of goals, and a highly competitive atmosphere. We were often the only non-Long Island team there, and were always treated well.

Adam had an excellent tournament. Despite his large frame, he had tremendous ball control, and took command in tight spaces. He rocketed in several goals, and came back hard on defense. He was one of the major reasons we did well, and everyone in the packed gym noticed his presence. Pierre had, as usual, an average tournament. He gave us what we needed -- a solid presence -- but did not clock nearly as many minutes as Adam.

Late Sunday afternoon, the awards were announced. The climax was Most Valuable Player. To our surprise and delight, the coaches and referees selected a Westport player.

They chose Pierre.

It was clear to everyone what had happened. The selectors obviously talked about "that black kid from Westport" – and because we did not play in the Long Island league, no one knew our players' names. So when it came time to present the award, someone simply guessed which was the better one.

What the hell. All those black boys from Westport look alike, right?

A far more enlightened experience involved the Martin Luther King Soccer Club, from inner-city Hartford. I can't remember how we connected, but I invited them to Westport for a Saturday-morning friendly match. Afterwards we had a little cookout: hamburgers, hot dogs, nothing fancy. The players on both teams were wary at first; after all, they'd just played against each other and, though only 12 and 13 years old, they knew that far more separated them than 60 miles of interstate highway. But they were also 12- and 13-year-old soccer players, all of them, and those common bonds enabled them to kick around – and fool around – with ease, very quickly. It took longer for us adults; we spent most of our time forcing small talk.

It was nice for our boys to get out of their comfort zone for a while. I would like to have done something similar the next season, especially in Hartford, but our schedules didn't mesh. I soon forgot about the Martin Luther King Soccer Club.

Over 20 years later, I found myself in Hartford on business. Walking near the state capitol I heard someone call my name, as a question: "Dan Woog?" Even at midday, Hartford is not the most happening place. The street was deserted, except for one well-dressed black man.

"Are you Dan Woog?" he repeated.

"Yes," I said. On my home turf I'm not good remembering faces and names; in downtown Hartford I was helpless.

The man came nearer. "I'm sure you don't remember me," he said. "But a long time ago I coached a soccer team. You invited us to Westport, and we had a little picnic. That was just about the nicest thing that ever happened to us, and I've never forgotten it. I just want to thank you again."

I was stunned. For over two decades – through four presidents, a few wars in places like Grenada and Iraq, the fall of disco and the rise of rap – this man had remembered a tiny gesture we had made. Not only did he recall the cookout, he remembered where we were from, and my odd-sounding name.

We chatted a bit, then went our separate ways. For the rest of the day, however, I had a smile on my face. And how interesting and symmetrical, I thought, while that game and picnic 20 years earlier might have been one of the nicest things that ever happened to his team, his recollection of it and of me had at long last become one of the nicest things that ever happened to me in youth soccer, too.

One more nice thing happened to me on a recent Sunday morning. Actually, it's every Sunday morning, all spring and every fall. A number of former players rise early, walk the dog, finish whatever chores must be done, then head off to a soccer game. They arrive in typical Fairfield County vehicles – Lexuses, Jeeps, Lincoln Navigators – not the bicycles, mopeds and VW Beetles they drove when they were younger. At the field they pull soccer jerseys over their shoulders (wider than before) and stomachs (bigger). They slip into soccer shoes – staying loyal to the same brand they wore as kids – and stretch.

This is Westport FC, our town's entrant in the Shoreline Adult Soccer League. They are now an "O" (Over) team – Over-30, to be precise – rather than a "U" team (as in Under-16). However, little else has changed. Their ages range from exactly 30 (one man waited impatiently all May for his birthday to arrive) to 40-plus. They know exactly how to play the game -- years in Westport and college (and, in one or two cases, the pros) have taught them that. They can't always make the runs they know they should, of course, and from time to time they can't quite reach a ball they used to always get to, but those are minor matters. They are playing the game they love, they play it correctly and with class, and for a few hours every Sunday morning life doesn't get much better than that.

Their wives and girlfriends often come, some toting young children and all the blankets, coloring books, miniature soccer balls, strollers, sippies and whatnot that come with little kids, but those few precious hours every Sunday are the guys' time. Win or lose – and they still win far more than they lose -- when the game is over, they sit wearily down and replay the game they've just played. They rag on each other for mis-traps and missed shots; they second-guess their own strategy, and compute how many more matches they must win (and who must beat who in other matches) in order to qualify for the post-season tournament. They talk about business and movies and family too – and ive vicariously through the tales of the few single guys' previous night's adventures – but somehow the discussion always swirls back to soccer.

I cherish those Sunday mornings. The Westport FC players are still 10,15, even 20 years younger than I, but nowadays they seem like peers. After all, we are all Over-30. So we sit and drink beers – it's okay, they're legal now – and laugh and bullshit. They are men now, but they're still my boys. And no coach could ever ask for any better combination than that.

TIME "OUT"

But enough about the players and parents I've worked with over the years. What about me? I've shared plenty of interesting stories so far, yet have not written word one about my personal life. You might be wondering why I have never mentioned a wife or girlfriend.

There is a good reason: I don't have one. And that is perfectly normal – perfectly normal, at any rate, for a gay man.

It took me a long time to be able to write a line like that. In retrospect, I know I have been gay all my life. And even before I knew I was gay, I knew I was "different" from other boys. In some ways, that difference helped make me who I am. My passion for soccer derives in part, I am sure, from an inner desire to prove that being gay does not mean I cannot run and kick and jump and tackle and sweat and enjoy victory and agonize over defeat the same as any straight guy. I am just as certain that growing up gay, while also playing and coaching, drove me deeper into the closet than I should have been, kept me there longer than I should have stayed, and made me, for many years, the homophobic person that I was.

Here is that story.

If you believe the research statistics, in my career I have coached several dozen gay soccer players. I am no mathematician, but I can figure out what 10 percent of the total number of players I've worked with is.

In all that time, not one boy has even hinted he might be gay. In subsequent years, of course, I have learned that former players indeed are. Some I suspected; others I never would have imagined. I know there are many others I do not know about.

During much of that time, I never revealed my sexual orientation to my players. They might have guessed – I was unmarried, I lived alone, I did not date women – and the older I got, the more the rumor mill probably churned. But I never brought it up, and no one ever did in my presence either. On my soccer teams, "don't ask, don't tell" was alive and well.

A number of years ago I finally came out of the closet – the locker room closet, as well as the many others I cowered in. The vehicle was my weekly column in the *Westport News.* Though soccer represents an important part of my life, I make my living as a writer.

I have been identified with both soccer and writing since before I was a teenager. In elementary school I was one of those teacher's pets who loves to see his words posted on the bulletin board, in the class "newspaper" and anywhere else anyone might notice. I was never a particularly good athlete, but Westport, Connecticut had a youth program for fifth graders as far back as the early 1960s, and I gravitated to it. The game was fun, and more importantly it did not involve trying to throw or hit a ball, so I stuck with it. Our junior high schools fielded interscholastic soccer teams, and those became my ticket to sports status.

Still, I would have had to be a much more gifted player than I was to break into Staples High School's starting lineup in the early 1970s. The Westport school's program was among the best in the nation. During my senior season our team allowed just two goals, and won the second of what became a national record five consecutive state championships. I watched the goals and glory from the bench, happy to hide my rapidly growing anxieties about sexuality in the welcoming blanket of teammates and friends who were well-respected, hard-working, high-achieving, intelligent and creative jocks. They dated girls, I reasoned; I did not, but I hung out with them. We all were jocks. So obviously I could not be gay. No way. Right?

I had even less chance of playing soccer at Brown University, a perennial national contender. So I settled for second best: covering the team for the school newspaper. To further embed my jock bona fides, I joined a fraternity. It was not the most popular thing to do in the'70s, especially for a self-styled liberal at one of the most free-thinking campuses in the country, but more important than my independence was being viewed by others as a straight man. In fact, being myself was the last thing I wanted. On graduation day I breathed a sigh of relief that no one had ever asked why I was the only frat man at Brown who never dated.

A job offer brought me back to my hometown of Westport. Social life in suburbia can be limited even for straight people, but coaching soccer provided plenty of challenges and enormous satisfaction. Happily, I was also pretty good at it.

I organized youth teams, which I and several others soon formed into the Westport Soccer Association. Over the years my teams won numerous state championships. I joined the coaching staff at my alma mater, Staples High – still one of the best high school programs in the United States. I set up all those overseas trips I spent the better part of this book describing. I was selected State Youth Coach of the Year in 1980, and National Youth Coach of the Year a decade later. All along I continued my soccer writing, winning awards for my coverage of youth sports. I traveled to World Cups and Olympics, and met Pele. Soccer was very, very good to me.

My coaching career taught me a great deal about adolescents: how they think, what they dream, who they are. Spending time at Staples gave me insights into high school education, so during the 1993 gay and lesbian march on Washington I attended a reception hosted by the National Education Association. A series of fortuitous meetings there led to the publication of my first book, *School's Out: The Impact of Gay and Lesbian Issues on America's Schools.*

My research included interviews with nearly 300 teachers, administrators, students, guidance counselors, nurses, librarians – and coaches. An openly gay football coach and a lesbian volleyball and lacrosse coach spoke eloquently about the coming-out process, highlighting its effect not only on them but also their athletes and, ultimately, their entire schools.

The more I spoke with these courageous men and women, the more I recognized that by not being out, I was doing all my soccer players – gay and straight – a disservice. Every afternoon at practice I preached honesty, yet every time I switched pronouns when mentioning something as mundane as with whom I had dinner or saw a movie, I lied. Every day I preached tolerance, never hesitating to halt training to address racial, ethnic or religious slurs, yet my rabbit ears turned deaf whenever I heard the words "gay" or "fag." Every season I stressed respect for others – teammates, opponents, spectators, even (god help us) referees – yet my actions clearly showed I did not respect myself. Every player looked up to me as a role model for sportsmanship and fair play, for compassion as well as competition, for the importance of education and the arts along with athletics. Yet in the area in which I might be the most important role model of all – proving that a man could be both macho and gay – I stood frozen with fear.

Ever so slowly, I inched out the closet door.

Midway through writing my book on gay issues in education, I gave a talk in our school library about the project. Over 300 students attended, the most ever for such a program. (I hold no illusions why: Homosexuality is far more enticing to teenagers than chemistry or the War of 1812.) I discussed the process of research, writing and publishing as much as I did the book's content, yet of course every question centered around gayness. I had promised myself before I began speaking that, if asked, I would say I was gay. Several students came close – especially the football player who challenged, "I got something personal to ask you," but then backed off with "I'll talk to you later" (he never did) – yet no one dared pop the "Are you...?" question. Suburban boys and girls are too polite.

During the session I mentioned that gay-straight alliances were popping up throughout Massachusetts. Immediately afterward, several girls asked me to help start one in our school. A straight teacher, Ann Friedman, agreed to work with me; our principal soon gave her okay. Within a few weeks our group had 20 regular members.

I grew more and more confident about coming out. In late May I was ready. I decided to do it in "Woog's World," my weekly newspaper column. The day before it appeared, members of our gay-straight alliance chatted about what we had accomplished in just a few months of existence. Someone commented, "I feel bad no one's been comfortable enough to come out here yet."

After a brief pause, I jumped in. "Pick up the paper tomorrow morning," I said simply. "Read my column." Instantly they got it. One boy, sitting in the front row, stared at me in awe. I knew then that, regardless of the fallout, I had made the right decision.

The next morning I was nervous, yet excited. I walked into the cafeteria – the student hangout – and felt a buzz in the air. In those days every kid scanned the paper for two reasons: to see if his name was in the sports section, and to make sure it was not in the police reports. Someone, I was sure, had stumbled onto my juicy piece, and alerted the rest of the high school. Yet no one had a clue what to say, or how to act. I looked around; 50 or so Stapleites either stared right through me or glanced away.

Suddenly the popular and respected soccer captain walked over and stuck out his hand. "Great column, Dan," he said. "I'm proud of you."

That broke the ice. For the rest of the day, students approached me. Some complimented the piece; others patted my arm as they walked by. A few just smiled – friendly smiles, not mocking. I made contact with people I had never spoken to before. I learned about so many gay and lesbian relatives, I felt like saying, "Okay, if you want to talk about an aunt or uncle, line up here; a cousin, over there. If it's a sibling or parent, I'll see you right now."

The funniest moment occurred when a guidance counselor approached while I spoke with a small group of students. "As long as we're sharing secrets, I've got one to tell you," she said. "For years, I've been trying to get you into bed. Now I finally know why I couldn't!" Then she walked away, leaving several dumbfounded high schoolers in her wake. "Hey, adults talk about sex too," I told them lamely.

The good feeling continued for days, with the soccer athletes among the most enthusiastic. Congratulations poured in; current players spoke to me in person, while others from the past called, wrote letters and e-mailed. "It's cool" was the main gist. "You're a good coach, we like you, and now we know a little more about you." The head coach of the varsity team told me how glad he was that I could finally be myself. I got a similar message from my former high school coach, 80 years old and a man I revered so much I still could not address him by his first name.

Only two current parents phoned; both were complimentary. One man said my column had allowed him to have the kind of honest discussion with his boy that every father always hopes for; the other said that that night they'd had the best dinner table conversation ever. Both men ended their calls the same way: "Thanks for coaching my son."

The father of a former player called. His four sons always told him he was homophobic, he said; his gut reaction to my column convinced him he might be. But now he wanted to talk with me and learn about homosexuality. I brought him books, and answered his questions. Months later, he told me he was a changed man.

I expected soccer people to be, if not accepting, at least not intolerant. After all, the game attracts a certain type of creative, intelligent, worldly person. I was less sure about the reaction of athletes and coaches in other sports, who at the time I believed to be less – well, creative, intelligent and worldly. Yet they too went out of their way to let me know that, even if they did not delight in the news or want it for themselves or family members, it did not change our relationship one bit. Football, basketball, baseball and lacrosse players complimented me on my "guts" (how's that for an athletic metaphor!), while coaches of those sports said it gave them a bit more insight into the person I am. The closest thing to a negative response came from a football coach, who happened to be reading my piece the moment I walked past his office. He looked up as if he had been caught masturbating, but immediately said, "Hey. If that's what you are and that's what you want, it's fine with me." I could not have asked for more from him.

The fall junior varsity season began. I did not stand on a soapbox, preaching about homosexuality and homophobia when I should have been teaching techniques and tactics. But I did not shy away from the subject. If someone asked why there was no training Friday, I told him: I would be attending the National Lesbian and Gay Journalists Association convention. If the T-shirt that made its way to the top of my drawer and into my gym bag happened to bear the logo of a gay pride parade, I wore it. And if a player wandered, inadvertently or not, onto the rocky terrain of gay issues, I met him there.

One day a boy tried to explain why a certain teammate was disliked. "It's always been that way," he said. "Even in elementary school, we had a TIAF Club."

"What's that?" I innocently asked.

Suddenly the player looked stricken. He opened his mouth, but was literally unable to speak.

"Come on," I prodded. "It can't be that bad. What's 'TIAF'?"

Finally, staring at the ground, he mumbled, "Tim Is A Fag."

"Well," I said, "I appreciate your telling me. Kind of makes you think about the power of words, doesn't it?" At last, grateful to be let off the hook he'd hung himself on, he looked up and nodded.

Another time the varsity players went through the traditional handshake line after an important victory over their archrivals. (This tradition consists of players on both teams racing past one another, saying "Goodgamegoodgamegoodgame" without meaning one bit of it.) A boy on the other team who had had a particularly difficult afternoon muttered "faggot" at one of our players. He had been outplayed, and in his frustration that was all he could do.

I reacted immediately. "No, I don't think he is," I said. "I'm pretty sure he likes girls. I'm the one who likes guys." The stunned boy's jaw dropped; he had no idea how to respond. The players on our team roared and high-fived me.

The following summer I took 15 players to the Netherlands, Denmark and Sweden. They played hard and well, and improved immensely; five straight times we beat or tied excellent European teams. But perhaps the most memorable moments took place off the field.

During the Gothia Cup in Gothenburg, players are housed in schools. Each team sleeps on cots in its own classroom. As can be expected when a group of 16-year-olds spends a week in close quarters, the air gets ripe. Nonetheless, it is a rare opportunity for team bonding – and unexpected encounters.

The team in the next room, from North Carolina, was sponsored by a religious organization. In between practices and matches, they held prayer meetings. Several zealous members handed religious tracts to our players. They were trying to save souls, and guess which group of sinners needed saving the most?

At breakfast one morning a boy on our team asked mischievously, "Dan, are you gonna say anything to those guys?"

"What do you mean?" I replied.

"You know, all that shit they're saying about gays – aren't you going to do anything about it?"

"Well, I'll tell you what I'm *not* going to do," I said. "I'm not going to get into a big brawl just so you can watch!" He looked disappointed.

That was the end of that – I thought. Two days later, though, the same boy approached me privately. "Dan," he said. "I finally went up to those guys from North Carolina."

"And...?"

"Well," he continued, nervously but proudly, "I told them they had, you know, every right to think what they want about stuff. But I told them they shouldn't diss gay people, because they probably don't know much about them. Besides, they don't know who they're offending."

"That's great!" I said. "But why'd you do it?"
He smiled. "I told them I had a friend who was gay."

My first instinct was to say, "That's so sweet!" But I restrained myself. He probably would have thought that was a little too faggy.

A couple of years later, with a different team in Europe, another boy approached me. He wanted to talk about a personal problem.

The way he said it made me think he was ready to come out to me. I was stunned – and worried. I had not considered he might be gay. As bright as I consider myself to be, I had never planned my response if a player came out while I was coaching him. And I was already late for a meeting.

"What is it?" I asked, an edge to my voice.

"Well, this chick I'm hooking up with here – she's a pretty bad kisser. What should I do?"

Yikes! This was far tougher than I imagined.

I reached deep into my bag of tricks. "It's all about communication," I began. "Why don't you talk to her? Tell her, 'You know, let's try this...' or 'What I really like is...'" I prattled on for a few minutes about the importance of talking with your partner about everything. He thanked me for the advice, then headed off to his woman.

I have no idea if it was a good answer or an idiotic one. Talking to teenagers about sex is no adult's forte. But that's not the point. What counted was: This 16-year-old got it. He understood that life is not about guys and guys, or guys and girls; it's about who you love (or, in his case, who you're hooking up with).

And when he returned that night, he gave me a big thumb's-up.

In 1995, in what was believed to be the first event of its kind anywhere, I presented a workshop on homophobia at the National Soccer Coaches Association of America's annual convention in Washington, D.C. Seventy-five college and high school coaches came to my session, out of a total convention attendance of 3,500.

The number did not disappoint me. I am sure many coaches did not make my workshop because they were worried about being seen; a concurrent session featuring the national team coach drew many others. But the ones who came proved what I strongly believe: This is an important topic, one that must be discussed. Seventy-five people, after all, had never gathered before to discuss homophobia in soccer.

The Moonie-owned *Washington Times* had predicted that my presentation would be the most controversial of the entire convention. They quoted one person as wondering why the topic needed addressing at all. "It's a bit like a talk on the Bosnian conflict at a shoe salesman's conference," the please-don't-quote-me-by-name coach said, managing in one fell swoop to give short shrift to soccer, homophobia, Bosnia and shoe salesmen.

Earlier, when the reporter had asked my reaction to that quote, I said I disagreed. I told him, "If we coaches are truly the people we say we are – teachers and educators concerned about the physical and emotional growth of every child we work with, straight and gay – then this is a topic we can't ignore." But the reporter chose not to print that.

The entire piece was negative, but I used that to my advantage in the introduction. "I could say, 'What do you expect from a paper owned by the Moonies' – but I won't," I began. "That would stereotype every Moonie based on what I've heard, not what I know. There might even be Moonies in this audience. I don't know who you are, or what you look like. That might embarrass you, if you don't want your Moonieality made public. After all, most people in America don't like Moonies. They don't want their kids to be coached by them. And they certainly don't want them to grow up to *be* Moonies!"

I had hoped to create a panel involving several openly gay coaches and athletes, nicely balanced among gender, age and geography. What I found was that those people willing to talk were unable to go to Washington, while those who could be there were unwilling to speak publicly. So I gathered four "life stories," and presented them myself. Then I introduced a college coach active in both the Gay Games and the International Gay and Lesbian Football (that is, Soccer) Organization. He spoke honestly – though with great trepidation – about why he was not out on his campus.

After our presentation, audience members asked questions. One man said, "I coach at the high school level. Doesn't a girl going on to college have the right to not play for a lesbian coach, and not play with lesbian teammates?"

"Let's turn the question around," I replied. "Would you get up in a public meeting and ask, 'Doesn't a girl have the right not to play for a black coach, or with Hispanic teammates?' You'd *never* do that – and if you did, you'd be crucified. Furthermore, what happens if she chooses a college because, she thinks, the coach is not a lesbian and there are no lesbian players? After she graduates and gets a job, chances are she'll have lesbian co-workers – maybe even a lesbian boss. How is she going to get along with them if she never learned those lessons earlier? The issue is not whether she has the right to play with lesbian teammates or for a lesbian coach, but why that's a problem for her."

The next query came from an athletic director. "I understand everything you're saying, but why do you have to talk about it?" he asked. "Why can't you just let it be?"

I answered that the issue exists whether it is talked about or not, so it is far better to bring it into the open than bury it. "If a player on your team shuts himself off from his teammates because he's scared they'll find out his secret, you're not going to have the best team possible," I explained. "And if there's something tearing your team apart, like rumors flying around about a player and you don't even know it's an issue, you're not going to be a very effective coach."

It was a good ending to a remarkable day. Several dozen coaches had their eyes opened, their horizons broadened. There was plenty of information presented, lots of honest give-and-take. My only surprise was that no one approached me afterward to come out – as gay, or a Moonie.

Which brings us to the present. The Staples High School gay-straight alliance continues to meet weekly. The longer it exists, the deeper it integrates itself into the fabric of the school, and the less often its posters are defaced. In addition, coming out has freed me as a writer to become both bolder and more honest. That is not merely a guess; several people have told me, "Dan, your columns are getting really good!"

As an openly gay soccer coach – and, since 2003, the varsity coach, only the third in our program's storied 54-year history -- I am happier, healthier, even more successful than ever before. I have the respect of my athletes, colleagues and – most importantly – myself. I look forward more than ever to every single moment I spend on the field. And although coming out is a life-long process, I no longer do it alone. Every year a new player on my team makes a homophobic comment; every year the older players race over, haul him aside, and explain life to him. Every year I watch as the young player's eyes grow wide – and watch him grow up.

And, after all, aren't those qualities – honesty, integrity, personal growth and being true to one's self – the heart of what youth soccer coaching is all about?

ABOUT THE AUTHOR

Dan Woog is a Westport, Conn.-based soccer coach, writer and educator.

In 2003 he was named head coach at Staples High School – his alma mater. In his first nine years the Wreckers won four league championships, and one state title. They reached the state finals two other times, amassing an overall record of 140-32-16. The high school's highly acclaimed website is www.StaplesSoccer.com.

Dan has been named Coach of the Year by the National Soccer Coaches Association of America (youth level), Connecticut High School Soccer Coaches Association, Connecticut Junior Soccer Association, and Fairfield County Interscholastic Athletic Conference. In 2000 he was inducted into the Connecticut Soccer Hall of Fame.

A graduate of Brown University, Dan has written thousands of newspaper and magazine articles, and been published in *The New York Times, Sports Illustrated* and *USA Today.* His 16 books include *Jocks: True Stories of America's Gay Male Athletes* and the sequel *Jocks 2: Coming Out To Play.*

He is a nationally known speaker, and appears often on radio and television (including a memorable stint on "The Daily Show with Jon Stewart"). He blogs daily about life in his hometown, at www.danwoog06880.com. The Staples High School website is www.StaplesSoccer.com.

Made in the USA
Charleston, SC
26 February 2013